All We Have Is Today

a story of discovering purpose

MICHELLE WULFESTIEG

ISBN-13: 9781499106862
ISBN-10: 1499106866

This book is dedicated
To my mother.
The strongest woman I know.

"*When it seems as though there is no hope, prayer is about invading the impossible. This book is a powerful testimony of how God is the Almighty Healer, capable of restoring the mind, body, and spirit so that we may discover his true purpose for our lives.*"

—Jack Hayford, bestselling author and former president of Foursquare Church International.

"*This book inspires us to think beyond what is possible, that there is a reason for everything, and that the veil between life and death is much thinner than we think—and that we should be thinking about that much more than we are.*"

—Nick Gilhool, executive casting director of the hit Showtime documentary series, "Time of Death."

A NOTE FROM THE AUTHOR

I have based this book on my personal experiences and have tried to recreate events, locales and conversations from my memories of them. In order to respect their anonymity, in a few instances, I have changed the names and characteristics of those who have touched my life.

TABLE OF CONTENTS

INTRODUCTION

Sometimes, we become trapped in the most ordinary places. For me, I was trapped in my bed—a place I thought would always be safe—as I struggled to survive a stroke. I was eleven years old. The next stroke came when I was twenty-five. It was worse. Catastrophic in fact.

After being diagnosed with a lesion in my brain, enduring radiation treatments, and losing the use of my right side, I had to learn to do life all over again. But more important: I had to learn to love myself again, and learn that God loved me.

When people are faced with a life threatening illness, they often struggle with their faith or become more deeply connected to God. My journey included both. When my nightmarish journey began, at the age of eleven, I couldn't understand why a loving God would do something so awful. What had I ever done to deserve this pain? As a teenager, thoughts of suicide filled my mind. As a young adult, I believed no man would ever love me. And overall, I never felt good enough, as if my disability prevented me from ever becoming a whole person. Yet something inside me knew that all of these feelings were false. In the depths of my soul, I knew that if I chose to believe the feelings, then those negative notions would indeed become my reality.

Still, it took many years before I finally discovered God's purpose for my life. And when I did, I realized that my stroke journey had been preparing me all along for a life of ministry dedicated to serving the dying. That's one of many important lessons I learned: that no matter what we go through, God can use it as a preparation time for us to grow into the people he has planned for us to be. Whatever we are faced with, we can be assured that God is grooming our hearts to do his work.

While my experiences are unique, I've discovered the principles that I've learned and lived through are universal to us all. My story could very well be your story. A story of perseverance. A story of believing and achieving. A story about God's amazing love, even when it seems he has abandoned you.

I don't know why things happen. Who really does? But I do know that everything happens for a reason. Even when I couldn't see the bigger picture, I had to trust that God was, and is, at work. Only when I developed a sincere level of dependence on the creator of the universe was I able to move forward.

You can move forward too. God loves you. He wove you together in your mother's womb. He created you uniquely and he has a great purpose for your life. So go out and live. Be strong. Be bold. Become all that you are meant to be. And know that God has you, and he is moving you forward to the exact place you need to be. You just have to trust him.

1

SMASHED TO PIECES

As the wind howled on a blustery, mid-December night, I awoke from a fragile sleep. A full moon beamed through my blinds and cast shadows over my canopy bed. I thought about school the next day. It was 1993. I was eleven and in the sixth grade. My class was in the middle of an art project, creating face masks out of papier mâché. I enjoyed art and especially this project.

What colors should I paint my mask? I wondered.

I rolled from my stomach onto my back and stretched, pointing my toes downward and raising my hands over my head. I held my breath and stretched more deeply, when suddenly a *whooshing* started. Loud pulsations began to thrash inside my skull like waves crashing against a rocky shoreline.

Yet this sensation was not abnormal. It actually happened all the time. Like when I dove into the pool to fetch water rings, chased the boys on the playground for too long, or did a back flip off the monkey bars. Anything that required exertion would bring it on, so, as irritating as it was, I never thought much of the *whoosh*. I naturally assumed everyone experienced this phenomenon.

When I was seven, we had a huge trampoline in our backyard that I loved to jump on. But with each bounce, I would hear and feel a clicking sensation in my head. Up. *Click.* Down. *Click.* Up. *Click.* Down. *Click.* One afternoon while jumping with my friend Krista, I asked her, "Do you have that clicking noise in your head while you jump?"

"No!" she said. "You're crazy."

So I kept bouncing, thinking nothing of it until the *whooshing* started, which made me feel lightheaded and forced me to stop.

Other than that, talking about it never crossed my mind again.

As it always had before, this night I assumed the *whooshing* would eventually subside. But this time, the sound of my pulse—*whoosh, whoosh, whoosh*—pounding through my head became ever more intense the deeper I stretched and the longer I held my breath. *Whoosh, Whoosh, Whoosh, WHOOSH, WHOOSH, WHOOSH.* Until finally, the thundering *WHOOSH* became so forceful that it felt as if someone smashed my head against concrete. Overwhelming pain shot through me as I became nauseated and began to slip in and out of consciousness.

During my waking moments, my head pounded as though sledgehammers were ruthlessly, rhythmically, beating into my temples. Gone was the subtle noise in my head I had always been used to. In its place was a steadily knocking blare that was louder than the raging thunder on an aggressive stormy night, a sound so riotous that I could barely hear my own thoughts. *WHOOSH, WHOOSH, WHOOSH.*

Moments passed, or perhaps it was hours, as I tried calling for my mother. "Help! Mom, help!" But my voice, barely a whisper, was too weak for her to hear. I tried over and over, but still she didn't come. The more effort I made, the more powerful the bashing sledgehammers became.

"Ashley, help! Help!" I tried calling for my younger sister, whose bedroom was next door, but she, too, failed to hear my feeble cries.

In the darkness of my room, I struggled to sit up. But I quickly learned that any movement caused the throbbing to intensify so severely, that the sound in my head became deafening. I fell back onto my pillow helpless and defeated. Overcome with pain, I slipped into a realm of oblivion until the morning light when my mother came to wake me for school.

"Michelle, time to get up." My mother's strong, business-like voice floated into my head, competing with the thunder still rolling there.

I could feel her long hair brush my shoulder and smell a faint scent of coffee on her breath as she leaned over me.

I didn't respond. I couldn't. She started to gently shake me, singing her normal wake-up song when I had trouble getting out of bed. "Good morning to you! Good morning to you! You look like a monkey and you smell like one too!"

I barely opened my eyes as I moaned and whispered, "I don't feel good. I have a headache."

"Come on, Michelle, get up and stop playing around. You have to go to school, and I have to go to work."

As a recently hired fourth-grade teacher at my school, Mom was always on schedule, arriving each morning forty-five minutes before the bell rang at 8:00 a.m. Although she had us on a tight schedule, it wasn't always easy getting me and my sister ready for school.

I didn't respond.

"All right, you can sleep in for a few more minutes. But I'm leaving at seven."

I slowly tried to get out of bed, but every movement made the hammers intensify. Fifteen minutes later I heard Mom come back into my room. "Come on, Michelle." Her voice sounded irritated. "You were fine last night when you went to bed, so I know you're faking it. You aren't playing the sick card again. I know you do that. Now get up."

She was right. I always had trouble getting out of bed and would pretend that I didn't hear her when she would try to get me up for school. But today it was real. I took a deep breath to gather my strength, then in a soft whisper, I said, "I can't, Mom. My head hurts. It feels like hammers pounding on my head."

She sighed heavily. "Fine, I still have to feed the horses and get Ashley dressed. You have thirty minutes. If you're not ready by then, we're leaving without you."

As much as I wanted my mother to know how terrible I really felt, I could not explain the severity of the situation. All I could do was lie still, since even to move my jaw to speak caused the pain to strengthen. But I didn't want to miss school. Not today anyway. A fleeting thought passed through the pounding: *My face mask*. I didn't want to miss painting my face mask during class. So I gritted my teeth and swung my legs over the side of the bed. As I sat up, I immediately became nauseated. No way did I want to throw up in my room. I clamped my mouth shut and rushed to the bathroom down the hall. I made it to the toilet just in time, vomiting as violently as the throbbing inside my head.

Now my body tensed up. A small bead of sweat broke out across my forehead. And all I could do was curl up in front of the toilet and cry, hoping I didn't vomit again, wishing the pain would stop.

Vaguely I heard my mother's footsteps coming up our wooden staircase, which was right next to the bathroom. I began dry heaving.

"Are you okay?" Her voice now sounded softer, concerned.

"No. I threw up. My head hurts, Mom," I said through my tears.

"Oh, no! You must have the flu. Let's get you cleaned up and back to bed." She helped me stand, walked me to my room and tucked me in.

"Let me get you some water and aspirin."

She left the room and within minutes, returned holding an orange baby aspirin, glass of water, and a red Tupperware bowl.

"Take this. Drink the water so you don't get dehydrated. Here's your bowl."

I put the pills in my mouth and chewed. Then I washed them down with the water. Minutes later, everything resurfaced back into the red Tupperware bowl.

"Shoot, Michelle! This isn't good. Let's get you back to the toilet."

"I can't, Mom. My head! I'm sick. Take me to the doctor."

She took the bowl and left the room. I could hear her in the bathroom rinsing it out.

She returned to my room and put her hand to my forehead. "You have the flu. The doctors can't do anything for the flu. Get some rest, sweetie pie." Her hand moved to my hair and she gently ran her fingers through it. "Here is your bowl. Here is the phone. I hate to leave you home alone, but I have to go to work. I'll see if Lori can check in on you, and I will call you at recess, okay?"

I heard my mother's Mazda minivan pull out of our gravel driveway, leaving me alone with our golden retriever, Mickey. He stood at the foot of my bed, his sad brown eyes looking at me with concern, as if he knew something was wrong. I reached out to pet the top of his head, but the throbbing in my own head was too much to bear. I leaned back against the pillow.

"I'm sorry, boy."

He jumped onto the bed and plopped down against me. I rubbed his soft fur, and closed my eyes to sleep.

Sometime later I was awakened by the phone ringing. Mickey, still faithfully lying next to me, lifted his head. I reached for the phone and answered.

"Hi, Michelle." It was my mother. "Are you feeling better?"

"I just woke up. It's not better." My head felt as though it would explode and shatter my skull into a million little pieces.

"You have a really bad case of the flu. Have you thrown up again?"

"No."

"Have you had anything to eat?"

"No."

"Why don't you go downstairs and eat something?"

"I don't feel good," I whined.

"I know, but you need to eat. Go downstairs and make yourself a sandwich."

"K."

"Okay. Lori can't stop by today, but I'll be home soon." She paused. "I love you."

"Love you too."

I hung up the phone and closed my eyes again.

The morning light soon became the setting of the afternoon sun and my mom came home to find me still in bed. She helped me sit up and took my temperature. One hundred and one degrees.

"Wow. I'm sorry, Michelle. I know you don't feel good and it's never any fun when you're sick. Why don't you come downstairs and I'll make you some soup."

"My head hurts, Mom."

"I know, sweetie pie. Let's try getting some food in you and see if that helps."

As I sat at the edge of my bed with the worst headache I had ever experienced, I helplessly watched my mother lovingly and gently place my slippers onto each foot.

"I don't want you to slip down the stairs with socks on."

I never made it back up the stairs. The couch became my new bed and the family room became my new bedroom. I couldn't eat, and what I did eat I threw up. Even a tablespoon of Dayquil found its way to the surface.

The next day my mom left in the morning, saying, "I'm sure you'll feel better this afternoon." But that day—and for the next several days—the opposite occurred. Aside from that first day, our neighbor Lori had been checking on me regularly. Like my mother, she had also assumed that I had a really bad case of the flu.

By the morning of the fifth day, I could no longer walk, and I was so weak that I could hardly pick up the TV remote. I also had a horribly stiff neck and back, as if there were a sharp metal rod going down both sides of my spine. My mom decided not to go to work because she was worried. But she first drove Ashley to school and then stopped by the local market to pick up some more medicine.

When she returned, she walked to the couch to greet me. Quickly her face registered fear. She grabbed some blankets and wrapped me up tightly. Then she scooped me up, put me in the car, and sped to the only physician in our small high-desert town of Anza, California. She carried me into the waiting room and placed me in a chair until the doctor was ready to see me.

Dr. Crane, a crusty old physician with a high, raspy voice and a dirty white doctor's coat, examined me and asked me to describe my symptoms.

When I didn't answer, my mom replied, "Pounding headache, uncontrollable vomiting, stiff neck and back, a high fever, and sleepiness."

A look of alarm came over his wrinkled face. "She has all the symptoms of spinal meningitis. We need to get her to the hospital immediately. I'll call for transport."

But my mom insisted that she drive me to the hospital. "I'm a single mom," she told Dr. Crane. "I don't have a lot of money and I'm not sure my insurance will cover the cost of an ambulance."

As we went back out to the waiting room, my mom stopped at the receptionist's desk and asked to use their phone.

"Lori! This is Shelley. Michelle is very sick and I have to take her to the hospital. Will you pick up Ashley from school and take her home with you? We don't know what's wrong and we don't know how long it's going to be. So can she stay with you and your girls tonight?" She paused, then a brief look of relief flashed over her face. "Thank you, Lori. I'll call you when we know more."

My mom hung up the phone and turned toward me. Her eyes were filled with tears.

"Come on, sweetie." She picked me up and put me in the car, then we headed to the nearest hospital, which was forty-five minutes away. Living in a remote town nestled in the mountains above Palm Springs, modern conveniences such as grocery stores, malls, movie theatres, and health clinics were a long drive. I heard Mom once say they were all a thirty-mile trip.

During the long and twisting drive to the bottom of the mountain, she talked nonstop.

"You need to stay awake, Michelle. Don't close your eyes, okay, sweetie pie?"

But my eyelids felt so heavy. Just as I would let them close, she would yell, "Michelle! Don't go to sleep. Talk to me. Talk to me, Michelle! Tell me about what you want for Christmas."

"Girl Talk," I replied. A board game I had seen advertised on television.

"What else?"

"Rollerblades," I said.

"That sounds like fun. Remember when you first learned how to roller skate? You were four years old and we were visiting Grandma Taylor in Carson City. Your older sister, Devonie, met us there for Christmas, flying in from her mom's house in Pleasanton. Santa brought you your first pair of roller skates and Devonie taught you how to use them in Grandma's driveway. Remember that, Michelle?"

"Yes," I whispered.

"Remember when you turned ten and we had your birthday party at the roller-skating rink in Hemet?"

"Yes."

"Maybe we can do that again for your twelfth birthday?"

"I don't want to, Mom. I've already done that," I whined.

"Okay. What do you want to do?"

"I want to have a party at my house with all my friends."

"We can do that."

We continued to talk about the type of party I wanted. Would it be themed? Would there be boys? Who would I invite? What games would we play? Would there be a piñata? My mom just kept talking and asking me questions about anything and everything.

After an exhausting drive down a steep and winding road, we finally arrived at Eisenhower Hospital's emergency. My mom parked and carried me across the parking lot. She half walked, half ran. My arms were dangling helplessly at my sides, and I was struggling to hold my head up. I quickly tired and laid my head on her chest, listening to her heartbeat. I felt comforted by the smell of her skin. Winded and sweating, she stepped through the ER's automated front doors.

"Please help us! My daughter! Our doctor thinks it's spinal meningitis. He said we needed to go to the hospital. Please!"

I started whimpering.

"Michelle, it's going to be okay. You're going to be fine, I promise."

"I'm sorry but you will have to wait," the nurse said. "There are other patients whose needs are more urgent."

We sat in the waiting room and waited. Every so often my mother would look at her watch. Finally, someone called my name.

"I can't believe we've waited forty-five minutes," my mother muttered as she put me in a wheelchair and pushed me toward an examination room.

Back in the room we waited a while longer until a doctor came in. He asked some questions and looked me over. Then he ordered a CT scan of my head.

I should have been scared by the loud knocking noises in the CT machine, or become claustrophobic from being sucked into the large plastic tube where the nurse said they would take pictures of my brain, but I was too sick to care. After the testing, instead of taking me back to my mother, the nurses took me to another room and began to question me as if I had done something wrong.

"Did you hit your head, Michelle?"

"No."

"Did someone else hit your head?"

"No."

"Did you fall?"

"I don't think so."

"Did someone push you?"

"No."

"Did your mother ever push you?"

The way they were asking made me feel as if I should have been answering yes. With each answer they looked at me as though I wasn't telling the truth.

Finally, a nurse wheeled me to a special floor that she called "intensive care." I had my own room. I looked around. It wasn't as nice as my bedroom at home, filled with pink curtains and a floral bedspread. This room was bare and white and felt cold. I wasn't sure why I got a room without anyone else. I assumed it was because everyone else around me was dying. Outside the room I could hear all kinds of commotion. The sound of running feet, nurses yelling, "He's coding" . . . "Clear" . . . *beep* . . . "Clear" . . . *beep* . . . "Clear."

The noises frightened me and I asked a nurse, "What's going on?"

"A guy in a car accident passed away."

I realized then just how sick I was, and that I could die also. I hadn't even begun to live. How could I cope with dying?

"Mom?"

"Yes, Michelle?"

"Am I going to die?"

She hesitated before responding, "No, Michelle. You are going to be fine." But her voice trembled a little, and I knew that she was as scared as I was.

No one seemed to know what was wrong with me. One doctor said it could be cancer; another thought it might be worms in my brain. That really scared me! And people they called social workers kept coming into my room, making my mom leave, and then questioning me about her. Did she ever hit me, push me, shove me, hurt me?

I couldn't understand why they wouldn't believe me when I kept saying no.

Finally, a doctor came in my room and bluntly told my mom and me that I had suffered a cerebral hemorrhage and the cause of the bleeding was still unknown.

"What's a cerebral hemorrhage exactly?" my mother asked.

"Your daughter had a stroke."

My mom started to cry. "But she's only eleven. How could this happen?"

The doctor simply shrugged and said, "It's still inconclusive." I didn't understand what that meant, but I knew it couldn't be good.

My head still hurt, and everyone was making the rest of my body hurt while they prodded and poked. I could hardly move since I was hooked up to countless tubes. And just as I would try to sleep, someone would come in and start poking and prodding all over again.

I wanted to believe my mom was right when she said I wasn't going to die, but I wasn't sure I believed her when my dad walked into the room.

My parents had gotten divorced several months before and he had moved four hours away to Phoenix so he could "start over." Although I was glad to see him, it felt awkward. *Why did he have to leave?* I thought. While Dad was there, another doctor—he called himself a neurosurgeon—entered the room with MRI results. He showed us a bunch of pictures and said they showed a rare lesion on the left side of my brain. He called it "an Arterio-venous Malformation or AVM," and explained it was "a massive tangle of veins and arteries in the brain that lack the capillaries to slow the blood flow between the two, which ultimately causes hemorrhagic strokes. To complicate things further, Michelle's AVM is abnormally large."

This made no sense to me. I knew only that my head hurt, and by the tone in the doctor's voice, I knew it wasn't good.

"What does that mean?" I asked.

The doctor moved in closer and in a gentler tone said, "Imagine a giant ball of twine, or a ball of yarn, that is completely tangled with no beginning and no end. Now imagine that that ball of yarn is your veins and arteries inside your brain."

"Does my whole brain look like that?"

"No. Only a small portion, about the size of a sausage. Most AVM's are about the size of a dime to the size of a quarter, so yours is quite large."

"Is that what made me sick?"

"Yes. When your blood pressure rises or when you engage in strenuous physical activity, the veins and arteries will burst. Do you remember what you were doing when you first started feeling sick?"

"It was the middle of the night and I was stretching."

The doctor scratched his chin as though he were thinking.

"Can't we just cut it out? I want that thing out of my head. I want to go back to school and be with my friends," I said.

"Unfortunately, that's not an option. You most likely wouldn't make it. Your AVM is too large and too deep in the brain."

"What do you recommend that we do?" my mother asked.

"Our best option is three Gamma Knife radiation treatments, which can be scheduled over the course of the next several years at another hospital, better equipped to deal with such a rare diagnosis."

"How did this happen?" my mother asked as tears streamed down her face.

"The cause of AVM is unknown and occurs in less than one percent of the population. We do know that the condition is present at birth, although it may be years before the onset of symptoms," the doctor replied.

"What did I do wrong to make this happen to her?"

"Don't go there. There is nothing you did to cause this and you will drive yourself crazy if you think you did."

She buried her face in her hands, and started to sob.

The doctor continued, looking at my dad. "Now that the AVM has bled, it's likely to bleed again. She needs to start treatment next month."

"Is she going to die?" my father asked.

"If left untreated, it's very likely."

That moment marked the painful ending of my childhood. I was only eleven years old, but gone were now the carefree days of tetherball and recess, disappearing forever as the cerebral hemorrhage left me fighting for my life.

2

THE BEST CHRISTMAS PRESENT

I spent ten days at Eisenhower Hospital, and for the first time in my life, I realized just how many people cared for me. I received dozens of get well cards, metallic helium balloons, furry stuffed animals, and Christmas presents, all of which covered the walls and filled my white room with overwhelming color. My mom even bought me a bedside Christmas tree, which she decorated with mini ornaments, twinkle lights, and popcorn string.

Mom told me about people from all over the country putting me on their church prayer chains. I felt loved. And I felt better. My headache was subsiding and I wasn't in as much pain.

Yet when the sun went down and my mom went home and my dad left for his hotel, I became frightened, feeling abandoned and alone. I experienced horrible nightmares and would wake up screaming, calling for my mom, hoping she could hear me, begging for her to take me out of this strange place. The nurses would tell me to stop shouting, saying that I was disturbing the other patients, but I didn't care. I just wanted to go home.

One day our neighbor Lori brought her daughters, Krista and Jennifer, and my sister Ashley to visit. I was so excited to see them, I couldn't stop smiling.

"Look at you," Lori said. "You have that pretty dimpled smile stretching from ear to ear!"

Though I hardly had the energy to engage in chatty conversation, I enjoyed listening to their stories of horseback riding, fort building, and treasure hunting over the last few days. I wanted to go home so I could join them, and it made me sad to think that I had missed out on all the fun.

At one point in the visit, Krista, who was one year younger than me, gently lifted a chunk of my disheveled, unkempt hair, crinkled her nose, and said, "Oh my! We have to do something about this. Michelle, you need a shower. Come on, get up. I'll help you."

I looked at everyone else. They all looked so radiant. I felt embarrassed by my appearance. Other than a sponge bath, it had been nearly two weeks since my last shower. My curly blonde hair was dirty and horribly matted, my mouth tasted like a cat died inside it. Even I knew I needed to be cleaned up. But my headache had been so awful that I wouldn't let anyone, not even my mom, touch my head to brush my hair.

Krista, Jennifer, and Ashley helped me sit at the edge of my bed. Krista and Jennifer sat next to me, with one on either side, and placed the arm that was closest to them around their neck, while Ashley grabbed hold of the portable IV pole.

"What are you doing?" my mother yelled, clearly panicked.

"We're giving Michelle a shower," Krista replied.

"That's not a good idea. Sit back down. Let me call a nurse," my mom said.

"No, I want Krista to do it," I said.

The nurse came and helped me to the small shower inside the adjoining bathroom. "How do you want to do this, Michelle?" the nurse asked.

Krista butted in and said, "I'll help. Come on, Michelle. Don't worry. If you want, I'll get in the shower with you to help you stand up."

"Okay," I replied.

"Are you sure you don't want me to help?" my mom asked.

"No, Mom," I said. "I want Krista to do it."

Ashley and Jennifer stepped back as the nurse carefully removed my hospital gown so as not to disturb my IV while Krista stripped down to her birthday suit and adjusted the temperature.

"Okay, it's ready," Krista said as she stuck her hand under the showerhead to feel the water's warmth.

I carefully walked into the shower. It felt so good to feel the hot water falling on my skin. I closed my eyes to enjoy the moment, but quickly became dizzy, lost my balance, and began to stumble.

Without hesitation, Krista jumped in to catch me. "Here, hold onto this," Krista said as she placed both of my hands on the grab bar. "Don't let go and I'll wash your hair." She lathered my hair with shampoo and conditioner and scrubbed my arms with soap, trying to remove the tape marks where the tubes had previously been inserted while being careful not to disturb the tubes that were still in place. After the shower, I felt a million times better and I finally fell asleep without any nightmares.

A few days later, all of my extended family came to visit me. As a broken family reunited, we had an early Christmas gathered around my hospital bed where we opened gifts from one another and tried to make the best of a difficult situation.

On Christmas Eve, I begged the doctors to let me go home; I was worried Santa wouldn't know where to find me. Toward the end of the day, the doctor walked into my room and smiled brightly. "We're letting you go home."

I was being discharged.

I spent Christmas Eve in the comfort of my own bed, and on Christmas morning, I went downstairs to discover I had more presents than I could have imagined. I spent the best day with my mom, Ashley, my half-sister Devonie, and close friends as we celebrated the birth of Jesus, the gift of life, and the beauty of love. In spite of the frost, we planted my bedside Christmas tree in our backyard and prayed that it would grow to be mighty and strong. And although I was still very weak, my mother prayed the same prayer over me—that I too would beat this thing and grow to be mighty and strong.

3

KIDS JUST WANT TO BE KIDS

With the start of the new year I returned to the sixth grade, but because I was at risk of having another stroke, the doctors determined that I could no longer play sports or engage in physical activity. I didn't care what the doctors said. I loved sports. I was on the track team, played football with the boys at recess, and was the fastest girl in my class. I just wanted my life to return to the way it was before and put this whole experience behind me. So in spite of the doctors' warnings and the teachers' attempts to keep me on the sidelines, I played and went on being a kid like nothing had ever happened.

Still, as much as I wanted it to, my denial didn't last long. Several weeks after returning to school, I underwent my first radiation treatment. The doctors told me that the procedure would be "no big deal" and that I could go home the next day.

On a Friday morning, my mom and I left our house before the sun came up and headed two hours south down the I-5 to Scripps Hospital in San Diego. Gazing out the car window, I realized then that we were headed to San Diego to kill the *WHOOSH*.

At the hospital I met a team of neurosurgeons, who were all going to help with the surgery. A nurse put me in a hospital gown and had me lie on a gurney. My hair was pulled back and the nurse asked if she could remove my pony tail holder.

"I can do it myself," I replied.

As I removed the rubber band, it became stuck in the frizz of my curly hair. I yanked it and finagled with it until thick locks of tangled morning hair fell around my shoulders.

"I'm going to put some ointment on your head so you won't feel any pain, okay?" Before I could respond, the nurse rubbed numbing ointment on both of my temples as well as on two locations on the back of my head. I could feel the hair on the back of my head getting goopy. Minutes later, a doctor pulled out something that looked like an electric drill. Another doctor placed a large metal halo onto the top of my head and began screwing it in tightly. It was heavy and squeezed my brain.

"What's that for?" I asked, trying to sound brave.

"This is so we can get the exact measurements of the AVM to radiate. It has to be precise so we don't make a mistake and do any damage."

I swallowed hard, closed my eyes tightly, and gritted my teeth as I tried to stay strong.

Why didn't they tell me this would happen? I thought. I wasn't prepared for this. They told me it was going to be no big deal. This was a very big deal! I tried to be tough, but my stomach started to do somersaults and I couldn't control the tears as they streamed down my face.

As soon as I was semi-sedated, but never fully unconscious, the staff began to run an extensive battery of tests to prepare me for the radiation treatment. The weight of the halo prevented me from lifting my head, but with each passing moment it felt heavier and tighter and I grew more scared. As loudly as I could I began to scream for my mom. Although I couldn't move my head, I could certainly move my arms and legs, and boy did I. I kicked and punched at anyone who came near me. I got a good punch in at one doctor. He turned away quickly and I heard a nurse say, "That's going to be a shiner."

Since I wouldn't stop yelling for my mom, a nurse finally brought her into the room.

"Michelle, you have to calm down. You're making things harder."

"I don't care. I want to go home!"

The more my mom tried to calm me, the more I screamed to go home. I didn't want to believe all this was happening, and I thought that maybe if I threw a big enough tantrum, I would get my way. I didn't like what they were doing to me, I didn't trust them, and they were making me hurt.

Eight excruciating hours later I was finally ready for the actual radiation treatment, the Gamma Knife. It had taken that long for the doctors to determine the exact coordinates. By then my head was oozing blood and fluid from where the screws were piercing my skull. The nurses moved me onto a hospital bed and then wheeled me into a large, sterile, white room with a huge white machine that looked like a football helmet. The nurses picked me up, laid me on the table at the base of the machine, and instructed me not to move.

"We'll be behind that tinted window right there, Michelle. Now make sure you don't move."

The medical team left the room, leaving me by myself. The doctor's voice came on over a loud speaker and said, "Okay, Michelle, we're going to start now. Don't move."

At that point, the table slid into the machine, placing my head inside the large football helmet, where it shot rays of radiation into my head, targeted at the AVM—at least that's what they told me was going to happen. I couldn't feel the radiation, but I knew it was zapping my brain, trying to destroy the *WHOOSH* that was threatening my life. Within ten minutes the treatment was over.

I spent the night in the hospital for observation. My mom tucked me in. I said my prayers and she left for her hotel room. The moment I fell asleep, the nightmares began. Aliens had invaded earth and their space shuttle was the Gamma Knife machine. Inside the football helmet were little, slimy, green creatures that made scary, high pitched noises while smiling and rubbing their hands together as they started toward me. I was locked in the room with them alone. I tried to scream but nothing came out. I tried to run away but there was nowhere to go. I was backed into a corner, completely helpless. Slowly, they inched closer and closer, in unison squealing, "Come here, my child, so we can eat you like a little sandwich."

I awoke terrified, my hair drenched in sweat. I was scared and I didn't know where my mom was. She didn't tell me what hotel she was staying at and I refused to stop screaming until I talked to her. Fortunately, one of the nurses was kind enough to call every hotel in San Diego until we finally found her. My mom was able to calm me down a bit, although I didn't sleep much that night. I was anxious and I kept thinking about the actual radiation treatment.

In spite of the doctor's strict instruction, I knew I had moved.

4

JUNIOR HIGH DREAMS

On Monday I was back to school, trying to return to my daily routine. I was still weak but feeling more self-conscious than anything else. The screws they placed in my head left dime-sized holes that hadn't stopped oozing, and because I was embarrassed, I wore a red bandana every day to hide them. Soon my close friends were wearing bandanas as a demonstration of their support, and before I knew it, everyone else in the class was wearing one as well.

I lived in a small town with a population of three thousand people and went to a school where each grade had no more than fifty students. In fact, I would often hear the teachers comment that our school was one of the last remaining public K-12 schools in California. It wasn't uncommon for kids to ride their horses to school, and the older kids who could drive had to park in a dirt field across the street, alongside the teachers. That's how small Hamilton School was. And because of its size, most of my classmates were like brothers and sisters to me. We had known one another since kindergarten, and if something happened to one of us, everybody knew about it and everyone was there to support the person.

When sixth grade graduation came around, I was the class valedictorian. During my speech, I thanked everyone for the amazing love they gave me when I was sick, but more importantly, I spoke about all the exciting opportunities I hoped the future would hold. We were entering junior high and we were one step closer to fulfilling our dreams, whatever they might be.

Summer seemed to fly by, and I moved on from the trauma I had endured, or at least had filed it away in the back of my mind. My mom had a new boyfriend, Craig, a recent divorcee with two girls of his own who were around the same ages as Ashley and me. We spent most days with them, and we seemed to sense that one day we would be sisters.

At the beginning of August we all went on a camping trip together. We towed jet skis fourteen hours up to Lake Trinity in northern California.

"This place is like paradise!" my mom said. I agreed.

Our days were filled with hiking, fishing, jet skiing, and water rafting. At night we roasted marshmallows and camped in tents under the stars.

One morning, I emerged from the tent I shared with Craig's daughter Chay and noticed that I had a slight limp. I felt no pain; I just couldn't pick up my right foot. As the day went on, it grew worse. I wasn't sure what had happened, but I didn't say anything to anyone since I figured whatever it was would work itself out.

"What happened to your foot, Michelle?" my mom asked with a look of concern.

"I don't know. It just feels weak."

"Maybe you hurt it when you were inner tubing and didn't realize it."

I shrugged and went back to playing charades with my sisters.

The next day, though, I could barely walk. Not only could I not pick up my right foot, I couldn't even move my leg. Once again, I emerged from my tent, but this time my foot and leg dragged in the red dirt as I clung to my right thigh with both hands, forcing myself to move.

"What's wrong with my leg?" I cried. "It won't work!"

My mom was brewing her morning pot of coffee over the camp stove. As soon as she saw me, she came toward me.

"What's wrong? Why are you walking that way?"

"I don't know, Mom! I woke up this morning and I couldn't move it." I started to panic. "Why won't my leg work?"

"I'm calling your doctor. Come on, Michelle. Get in the car and we'll drive up to the store to use the payphone."

Craig, a late sleeper, emerged from his tent.

"What's going on?"

"Michelle's leg won't work! I have to call her doctor," my mom said, her voice filled with alarm.

"You call and I'll watch the girls."

My mom helped me into our Mazda minivan and we drove up through the wooded campground to the general store and pulled up next to the payphone. She rummaged through her purse until she found my neurosurgeon's business card.

"Hello. My daughter is Michelle Taylor. She had the Gamma Knife treatment about six months ago for her AVM. Yesterday she couldn't pick up her right foot, and today she can't move her right leg."

She paused.

"Hold on, she's right here. Let me ask."

She covered the phone with her hand. "Michelle, I'm on the phone with Dr. Fuller. He wants to know if you have a headache."

"No," I whined. "My leg just won't work. It won't work!"

"No, she doesn't have a headache," she said into the phone. She paused, listening to his voice, then turned to me. "Do you have feeling, Michelle?"

"Yes, I can feel everything, but I can't move my leg. I can't even wiggle my toes! It's like dead weight."

Mom spoke again into the phone. "She has feeling, but she can't move any part of her leg. It's like it's paralyzed."

She listened intently as tears began to well up in her eyes. She turned away from me and wiped at her face. Seeing her cry made me afraid and I began to wail, as I rubbed my leg with both hands and asked God to please make it work.

Although my mom had lowered her voice, I heard her say, "We can't come today. We're camping in northern California. Should I take her to the hospital? They have one in Redding."

She continued to cry and listen. "I'd rather go back to see you. You're familiar with her case. We will be there tomorrow morning."

She hung up the phone and hugged me tightly.

"We have to go home, Michelle."

"I don't want to!" I screamed as I pushed her away. "I don't want to go back to the hospital. I hate it there. I hate it!"

"We don't have a choice. I don't want to go either, but we have to take you to the doctor."

We got back in the minivan, and cried all the way back to the campsite.

My mom got out of the car immediately, while I stayed put. I didn't want to face everyone.

"We need to go," Mom commanded. "We need to get Michelle to San Diego as soon as possible."

Not only was I scared about my leg, but now I felt terrible for ruining our fun vacation. No one seemed to complain, but I still felt bad.

It took us fourteen hours to get home. The next morning we left our house at 5:30 a.m. so that we could be at Dr. Fuller's office in San Diego in time for his first appointment. He immediately ran some tests—fortunately, they weren't as painful as the head screws.

"Michelle has swelling and edema in the left side of her brain, which is most likely blocking the nerves that send signals to her right leg," he explained. He prescribed steroids and told me, "Don't worry. In a few months, you'll be running down the beach." Then he turned to my mother. "We're going to start her on physical therapy. In the meantime, though, go to a local medical supply store and buy a simple, athletic brace. It will help her with the drop foot until she gets her strength back."

Several weeks later, I started seventh grade. My phys. ed. class was the worst. I'd always loved to run and jump and play sports, but now I really wasn't allowed. So as I watched my classmates having fun, I had to sit out, feeling embarrassed and depressed. My teacher tried to make me feel better by making me his assistant. I tried to be positive about it, but my efforts seemed useless. This was yet another thing that I'd loved and lost the ability to do.

Dan was my new physical therapist. He was an odd, slightly over-weight man in his fifties who was bald except for the gray frizzy hair that stuck out from both sides of his head. Like Dan, the building where my appointments took place was equally peculiar. The office space, located in Hemet, about forty-five minutes from my town, had previously been a bank, so I would check in at the former teller's window and proceed to the back where all the exercise machines were laid out in the wide open. There were no private rooms, except for Dan's office, which was the vault that had previously housed millions of dollars, or so I imagined.

I quickly learned that Dan knew nothing about my condition and had never even heard of an AVM before. As a result, my mom brought him articles to educate him about my recent diagnosis. After a little reading, he became a self-proclaimed expert, which irritated me to no end.

"I know all about what's happened here. You have to exercise as much as possible, Michelle, if you want to get the use of your leg back. We need to get those muscles moving so that your brain can create new pathways."

"How do you know? You never even heard of an AVM before you met me!"

"True. But I know how the brain interacts with the muscles in your body. It is the command center for everything. If your brain is damaged, then sometimes your muscles won't know how to act. Through exercise and repetitive movements, though, the brain can learn other ways to bypass the damaged part so that your leg can work again. It's something called neuroplasticity. Luckily, the younger you are, the more neuroplasticity you have and the more likely you are to make a full recovery. You are only twelve, so your age is in your favor."

"Great. My leg doesn't work and I have brain damage. It's my lucky day!"

"Watch it, Michelle," my mother warned. I wasn't shy about copping an attitude and she never lost an opportunity to nail me on it.

I hated physical therapy. Not only did I believe that Dan wasn't knowledgeable enough to help me, but I was also the youngest person receiving treatment, which made me feel lonely and out of place. One day I was sitting across the room from another patient, a thin old man who was wearing a long-sleeved, red plaid shirt, brown pants, and a trucker hat, with his wife and cane at his side. I overheard Dan tell him that he was already too far gone and that he would probably never recover. Dan apologized and told him to keep his head up. I noticed the old man's plastic leg brace and his left hand lying motionless in his lap. Like me, the old man had suffered a stroke.

As the couple left the building, my heart ached for them. I understood their pain. Dan then came over to me and said, "I don't want to have to tell you the same thing. You are in a lot better condition than he is and you will get better. Just keep exercising and have determination."

Three days a week Dan would stretch my right leg, and then have me exercise on the bicycle and the stair-stepper. Sometimes he would exercise my right arm with the arm cycle.

"Why do I have to exercise my arm? It's not the problem."

"We're exercising it because I'm worried that you might lose use of that as well."

"You're crazy! Look at my arm. It's fine. I can move it perfectly," I said as I waved my right arm around, opening and closing my hand a dozen times. I couldn't believe him saying that I could lose the use of my right arm, on top of the loss of my right leg. After everything I had been through, that was the last thing I wanted to hear. I couldn't worry about my arm too. I was too busy focusing on Dr. Fuller's promise—that one day I'd be running down the beach.

5

THE SHOE LACES

As the weeks passed, the entire right side of my body lost more and more of its muscle. My mother called Dr. Fuller who said I needed to go to the hospital. So we drove the two hours back to Scripps Hospital in San Diego where I was admitted for what the doctors told us was a "setback."

As I lay in the hospital bed, my mom would grab both my hands and say, "Squeeze!" I did as she instructed; my left hand exerting full strength, my right hand rapidly losing strength. "Squeeze, Michelle. Please squeeze!" my mother pleaded with tears in her eyes.

The next morning I awoke in the hospital bed to find that I couldn't move the entire right side of my body. Two and a half months after I had lost the use of my right leg, I lost the use of my right arm. Dan was right.

Dr. Fuller explained, "The intensive radiation treatment Michelle had back in January seems to have damaged the motor strip on the left side of her brain. Unfortunately, it has caused permanent paralysis of her right side."

I listened to Dr. Fuller's words and knew immediately: it was my fault. Ten months before, during that horrible treatment, I had moved.

Did I mess up the doctor's coordinates? I worried. I felt ashamed and scared. But then I realized, even if I had, at this point it really didn't matter, because regardless, I was handicapped.

Dr. Fuller's promise that I'd be able to run on the beach felt like a dream faded. Not only could I not run, I couldn't do anything. I was totally dependent on my mom to care for me. I could no longer feed myself, button my pants, wash my hair, or tie my shoes.

And when I looked in the mirror I saw someone I didn't recognize. My face was swollen from the steroids and my hair was still falling out in chunks from the radiation. My image showed me someone I had never met before—and someone I didn't want to know.

I lost everything I knew about me. I overheard my mom and the doctor talking. They said that I'd have to relearn how to do everything, that I would have to find "a new identity."

I didn't want to find a new identity. I'd lost my old one and I wanted it back!

The worst part was that I realized I was permanently unable to run track, play softball, football, and all the other physical things I loved to do. I never really knew how much I loved doing them until I no longer could.

I cried a lot. I felt sorry for myself. I wanted to die and I contemplated killing myself. I thought God was punishing me for all the bad things I had ever done. Like when I teased the chubby girl on the playground and got suspended from school for calling her a whale. Or for the time I tried to run away from home on my bicycle because I wanted new parents.

When I returned to school, my friends now relentlessly teased and made fun of me. I was in a wheelchair with a big plastic leg brace, similar to the one I saw that old man wearing in Dan's office, and an arm sling to keep my dead arm from coming out of my shoulder's socket. One kid thought I was faking it and tried to push me out of my wheelchair to prove it to his friends. Fortunately, a girl named Deanne was there to defend me and pushed him away. After that incident, I refused to return to school in a wheelchair. It was difficult to walk, but it seemed to be a better option than the latter. Other kids would point and laugh, "Your face is so fat! I've never seen anything like it!" I hated the steroids. They made me ugly and I was so swollen that my entire body hurt to the touch. Instead of being picked first for the team during P.E., I was forced to enroll in adaptive physical education. In an instant I went from being the most popular girl in my class to a social reject.

I tried to find anything to keep me from feeling like a complete outcast. But that seemed impossible. The school made me switch to adaptive P.E. because they said I could no longer be the regular P.E. teacher's assistant. They said that the adaptive P.E. would help my condition.

How much worse can this get? I thought.

Coach Schroeder was the adaptive P.E. teacher and he was also the head high school football coach.

At least I get to work with someone cool. He was well liked by all the students, even the non-athletic type.

I learned quickly that Coach Schroeder had only one tone: yelling. Because there were no extra classrooms available, we met in a secluded corner of the library with the two other students in the school who had a physical disability; one was a quadriplegic, and the other had cerebral palsy. Unlike me, Adam and Tina had lived with their disabilities all of their lives, so adaptive P.E. was nothing new to them. I, on the other hand, was considered the newbie and I was still raw. This was so hard for me! And the only way I could handle it was to cry.

On my first day of class, Coach had to create an individualized exercise plan for me based on what I could and could not do. Mostly, Coach wanted me to focus on picking up things with my right hand. He wanted me to move my fingers and try holding a pencil since I was previously right handed. But I couldn't. I couldn't do anything with my right hand. It was lifeless. Dead.

"I can't! My hand won't work. I'm telling it to move, but it's not listening," I cried.

Coach Schroeder, who called everyone by their last name, yelled, "Taylor, if you don't bite that lip and toughen up, you'll be no good to anyone. Now stop feeling sorry for yourself and stop your crying." This only caused me to cry harder, and he threw up his hands and walked away, moving on to help Adam and Tina with their exercises.

During my first week of class, my shoelace came untied. "Coach Schroeder," I said. "Will you please tie my shoe?"

"Now this is something you're going to have to do on your own, Taylor. I'm not going to do it. You're going to try."

"I can't," I whined.

"Yes, you can. And you are not leaving here until you show me that you can do it."

"But we only have fifteen minutes left of class," I protested.

"I don't care. I will call your next teacher and tell her you can't make it. You are not leaving here until you learn to tie your shoe with your left hand."

Tears filled my eyes, spilled onto my cheeks, and fell onto the tattered carpet as I bent over my leg with my hands dangling over my untied shoe. Coach Schroeder squatted next to me and in a softer tone said, "Now stop that crying. You can do this."

"No, I can't. I *can't*." I gulped for air and kept my face toward the floor. "Why did this have to happen to me?"

"Taylor, I don't know why. All I know is that this is how it's going to be from now on. And if you want to succeed in life, you had better start trying to learn how to do things differently than you did before. Now, I am not taking no for an answer. You are not leaving here until you learn how to tie that damn shoe. Are you with me?"

"Yes," I sniffled.

"Let's do it then! I'll watch how you do it and then I'll offer suggestions. I will even try tying my own shoe with just my left hand to see if that helps. We'll do this together, okay?"

"Okay."

I took both the laces in my left hand, crossed them over, and placed the left lace under the right lace. He did the same.

"Now what?" I asked.

"Can you grab the laces with both hands and tighten them somehow?" He knew the answer was no, and I figured he was thinking aloud. "Hmmm." He paused, then said, "Can you wrap the right lace around your right thumb to pull it tight while you use your left hand to tighten your left lace?"

He demonstrated for me and I tried following his lead. It worked!

"Okay, now unravel the lace from your right thumb and use your good hand to make a loop with your right lace."

I did as he said.

"Good. Now with your left hand, can you take the left lace and wrap it around the loop, threading it under and through the second loop?" I watched as he demonstrated, creating a perfectly tied shoe.

"Wow, how did you do that?"

"I just showed you. Seriously, Taylor! Now it's your turn."

My first attempt was a failure. The second attempt almost worked. The third attempt, I did it! The tie was loose and sloppy, but I had tied my own shoe with one hand.

"See Taylor! I never want to hear you say that you can't do something ever again. You can do anything you put your mind to. All you have to do is try. And if that doesn't work, you try again until you get it right. You understand me?"

"Yes," I said, now smiling as I wiped the tears from my cheeks.

The bell rang. Coach Schroeder quickly retied my shoe so that it wouldn't come undone again and said, "We are going to practice this every day until you can tie those damn shoes with one hand and your eyes closed." He stood up. "Now get out of here. You don't want to be late to your next class."

6

SEARCHING FOR SOMETHING

At my first physical therapy appointment since the "setback," I limped into the office, my right leg fitted in a knee-high, orthopedic leg brace, my right arm lying motionless in a sling. Dan started toward me where I sat in the waiting room, shook his head, and said, "Come on, let's get you started," and led me back to the stretching table.

As the weeks went by, Dan would tell me that my physical condition was improving. Actually, one week he would say I was getting better, and the next week he would tell me I was getting worse. It was altogether depressing. Still, Dan always said how proud of me he was. He couldn't understand how a twelve year old girl could be so strong with such a burden. When he found out how I could tie my shoes with one hand, he was all the more impressed.

"Are you practicing writing with your left hand, since you were previously right-handed?" he asked.

"Yes. I hate it. Because I'm in junior high, I have to take lots of notes on what the teacher is saying. I have to tape my paper to my desk since I can't use my right arm to keep the paper from sliding away. It's just so frustrating. You can't even read what I write. My teachers keep saying it's okay and that my writing keeps getting better, but it's still hard."

"Well, that's great, Michelle. You are a very brave and very determined young woman," he said, giving me a wink.

I smiled at him and my right arm raised itself. I pointed to it with my good arm and said, "This is Fred."

Dan looked at me puzzled.

"My sister Ashley named it. Since losing the use of my right side, it has developed a mind of its own, and when I get excited or nervous, it raises in the air. Is that normal?"

"It probably has something to do with spasticity and nerves," he said as he began moving my arm, slowly at first and then more quickly to see if he could trigger the spasticity, which he did, causing my arm to violently begin shaking.

"My sister gave him a boy's name because he does what he wants and never listens to anything I have to say."

Dan laughed, which made me laugh. It made me feel a little better.

"Your sister is a wise girl. How old is she?"

"Ten," I replied.

"Well, I'll be!"

I didn't know what that meant, but he was smiling, so I assumed it wasn't bad.

After that, my physical therapy time with Dan became a little easier for me to handle—at least emotionally—until one day, several months into the therapy. I was having a terrible day and I couldn't seem to do any of the exercises Dan wanted me to do.

At the end of the session, when my mom came to pick me up, she and Dan began to talk about my condition as if I wasn't even in the room. I couldn't hold it in any longer, and once the tears started coming, they wouldn't stop. Dan patted me on the back, gave me a hug, and said, "I've been expecting this. It's okay, kid. Go home and take it easy." It was the first time I cried in front of him.

The second radiation treatment came exactly one year after the first and it was much easier to deal with because I knew what to expect. I would have a metal halo screwed into my head, be semi-sedated for eight hours so that the doctors could get the exact coordinates, and spend the night for observation. But this time, I promised myself that I wouldn't move. And I didn't.

Even though I had another radiation treatment, and even though my body didn't work the way I wanted it to, I still believed wholeheartedly that I would fully recover and that one morning, I'd wake up and my life would return to the way it was before. I would run on that beach. But even better, I'd be able to rejoin my classmates in P.E. My friends wouldn't tease me any longer. I'd go back to being the most popular girl.

But with each day that passed and nothing changed, I began to get angry. Mostly with God.

"Why me?" I demanded over and over of him. "Why did this have to happen to me? And why aren't you fixing it?"

I constantly heard at church that God loved me, but I couldn't see it. I couldn't understand how a loving God could be so cruel, and I hated him for it.

After I turned thirteen, I wondered if maybe God wasn't healing me because he wanted me to do better, to be a better person. So I went to church every Sunday and attended youth group consistently, because if I devoted my life to the church, then surely God would bless me with a miraculous healing. I made countless trips to the altar and had people pray over me there. But nothing changed.

A voice inside my head began to whisper, *You don't want to live this way. Your mom is tired of having to do everything for you. Everyone would be better off if you were dead. God doesn't even care. It would be so easy . . .*

I believed the whispers. I believed I would be better off dead. I wanted my battle to be over. I was tired. And it seemed all I could do was cry.

My mom appeared to have no sympathy. She offered to put me in counseling, but I refused.

"Michelle, you have to stop feeling sorry for yourself. I don't know why this happened, but it is what it is. You have to move on. Come on, let's go make cookies."

I knew that was her attempt to take my mind off myself. Most of the time it worked.

But I couldn't get past the sense that no one seemed to understand or care. The truth was that I was too scared to try to kill myself. I didn't like being in pain. And even though my circumstances stunk, I knew that I had better change my attitude if I wanted to move forward.

Slowly I resigned myself to the truth of who, or what, I had become. I started to accept that my circumstances were indeed my reality and that I would have to learn to make the best out of a bad situation. Instead of feeling sorry for myself and playing the role of the victim, I began to view myself as a survivor.

How I previously defined myself no longer fit with the person who was evolving within me. I knew that I was changing, but into what? I had no clue. It felt as if my life were in limbo. I didn't know or understand who I was and felt confused about my role in this world. I questioned what I was meant to do and spent a lot of time pondering my life's purpose. I always trusted that my health would remain intact, but now I realized that in life there was no promise of that. I knew that there must be some kind of higher power, with some bigger plan for my life, but I was uncertain of what that looked like.

It felt as if I were blindfolded in an unfamiliar room trying to find my way to the door. I couldn't see where I was going, and although I had a sense that I was going *somewhere*, there was nothing for me to hold on to. On top of feeling lonely and isolated, whenever I'd try to talk with my mom or any other adult, they'd just say, "Sweetie, you're thirteen. Every thirteen year old goes through this. It's normal."

But it didn't feel normal. And how could I be normal? The other kids may have been dealing with something, but they didn't have a dead right side added to it. There was no one to lead me, and in an effort to reorient myself, I turned to alternative homeopathic remedies that I thought might be able to cure my illness and my disability.

We lived near Idyllwild, a mountain town filled with hippies who were into that kind of thing. I had an older friend named Lisa, who lived down the street. She was seventeen and she would drive us to a store there called Lady of the Lake that was filled with incense, candles, tarot cards, astrology books, and information about how people can heal themselves. I also had a Spanish teacher whose wife sold essential oils along with herbal medicines.

Why not give it a shot? Nothing else has worked. What have I got to lose?

So I convinced my mom to spend thousands of dollars on various concoctions sold to us by people who promised healing and well-being. I even went as far as eating a vegan diet where I consumed nothing but homemade beet juice for a week straight. I had to cleanse my body, purging it from all the toxins that had built up over the years, or so we were told.

About six weeks into this whole process, my mom approached me. "Michelle, I know you want to be healed and I want the same. But do you really think this stuff is working?"

"Yes, Mom. I'm getting better. I am gaining the use of my right side back. I can move my arm now and I don't need an arm sling. Soon I won't need a brace either. It's awesome!"

"I know. But don't you think that is because you are young and have more neuroplasticity like Dan was talking about? All this alternative stuff just seems like hocus pocus and I really can't afford it."

"But don't you love me?" I asked.

"Of course I do. With all my heart."

"Then why would you stop? Please, Mom, I need to get better! You can't stop. You can't. Please!" I begged.

So as much as she clearly stressed that she didn't agree, she permitted me to continue my quest, holding on to some glimmer of hope that I may one day make a full physical recovery.

I came home one Saturday after having my fortune told at Lady of the Lake and couldn't wait to tell my mom all about it.

"Mom, the woman who read my palm says that I am an old soul with many past lives. She said that I am wise beyond my years and that I will grow up to be very successful and never have to worry about money. She said I will be healed from whatever illness I've been battling. She said I will get married and have two kids! Doesn't that sound great?"

Mom sighed, "Oh, Michelle, it sounds wonderful, but don't you know that those people aren't psychics? They are just telling you what they think you want to hear. I really wish you wouldn't spend your allowance money on that."

Psychics were the one thing my mom refused to pay for.

"Well, I believe it's real! Can't you just be happy for me?"

"I am happy for you. But this is just a phase. You are searching for answers right now. And I don't think you'll find what you're looking for in Idyllwild. I don't think you will be healed by essential oils either."

"I can't believe you just said that! You don't care about me. You just care about Craig!" (By this point he and my mom were married.)

"That's not true."

"Yes, it is! And now that Chay and Jenna are living with us, you care about them more than you care about me and Ashley because you're trying to show everyone what a great stepmom you are. You have a new family now, so what do you need us for?"

"Knock it off, Michelle."

I turned away and stomped up the stairs to my bedroom. "I hope you're happy, because I hate you!" I shouted before slamming my bedroom door.

My mom followed me up the stairs and gently knocked on my locked door.

"Michelle, let me in. I want to talk to you."

"I don't want to talk to you."

"Michelle, let me in now."

I unlocked my door and returned to sitting on my bed.

"You can't talk to me that way. I know you don't hate me, but those are very hurtful words. I am doing the best I can, Michelle. Don't you see that?"

I didn't respond.

"Hey, I have an idea. Why don't you go up north to visit Devonie? It will be a nice break for us both and the two of you can catch up. I'm sure she would love to see you."

My eyes lit up with excitement. "Really?"

"Yes. I will call her mom to make sure it's okay, but I think it's a wonderful idea."

The following week I was on a plane headed to Oakland for a long weekend with my half-sister. I was a little nervous because it was the first time being away from my mom since the diagnosis, but I would never let anyone know it.

Once I got to Devonie's house, I ate an entire box of See's Candy for breakfast, which wasn't the best idea. I spent the entire day throwing up.

The next morning Devonie came in my room and told me to get dressed. She was taking me to the mall and we were going to have our hair done.

"Okay. I feel a little better. Will you help me get dressed?"

"No way! Are you crazy? You're a big girl. You can dress yourself."

"But my mom always helps me."

"Well, I'm not your mom. So you're going to have to figure it out."

From that day forward, no one, not even my mom, had to help me get dressed again.

Several months later, toward the end of the school year, I was sitting in my social studies class doing a project where we were grouped in pairs. I was randomly matched with Tommy. Somehow we got on the topic of religion when Tommy told me he had given his life to God. Of course I was happy for him, but I couldn't help feeling my own sorrow for my seemingly failed relationship with Christ.

I explained to Tommy how I had once turned to God because of my AVM. Becoming a part of a powerful religion seemed the only cure. Time and time again I had prayed to be healed. I told him how I had gone stumbling to the altar, promising Jesus my soul and praying for the mercy of his healing hand.

"My prayers were never answered. I gave up on faith. The whole thing just didn't work for me."

"That's because you prayed for selfish things."

Tommy's words left me speechless; they felt like a lightning bolt to my soul. At that moment I realized my own arrogance, causing me to step back and look at my life from where he stood. Suddenly I understood that God doesn't exist solely to serve me, but instead, I exist solely to serve him. This life was never about me. I was designed by him and for him. I still didn't understand why God had chosen not to heal me, but he knew, and there had to be some purpose in that. Right?

That night I reached under my bed and pulled out my Bible. I dusted it off, since it had been there untouched for more than a year. I randomly skimmed through a couple chapters and read Proverbs 3:5-6, "Trust in the LORD with all your heart and lean not on your own understanding; in all your ways acknowledge him, and he will make your paths straight" (NIV). I immediately felt God's presence and began to cry. I couldn't pray though. It had been so long, I wasn't sure I remembered how. The only words that fell from my lips were, "Dear God." My mouth fell silent. And I sat in the silence, accompanied only by my salty tears.

I ran my fingers over the embossed letters of my name on the Bible's cover. Our family pastor gave it to me while I was in the hospital after being diagnosed with my AVM. In the empty beginning pages, my pastor wrote, "Stay close to God and he will stay close to you." It made me sad to read those words, because my relationship with God seemed so distant. I wanted to stay close to him, but I just didn't understand why he would do this to me.

As my fingers lingered on the cover, an incredible sense of fear came over me. I felt God's presence so intensely I began to think that if I became close with him again, he would punish me for all the times I'd ignored him. I began envisioning an angry, all-powerful God who would strike me with a seizure or another stroke.

Somewhere deep inside I always thought God was punishing me. He gave me this brain lesion and took away the use of my limbs as a means of some retribution. Then a vision flashed through my mind of me sitting in a wheelchair, being there permanently. *Someday I won't be able to care for myself and there will be no one there to help me. What then?*

That vision stuck with me for months. And I fed it by remaining isolated as much as I could. I would spend hours upon hours alone in my room, meditating, writing, looking for signs as to what might be next.

What is my path? Where am I going? How does God fit into all this? I needed answers. I needed resolution. I thought about my life up to where I was now at thirteen and the dark whispers began again in my mind, telling me to end my life, to quit, that I would never get answers and that life was too hard anyway. But another voice began to speak. This one was softer, kinder. It showed me the opportunities that still lay before me.

Maybe I could still live a full life in spite of my physical limitations, I thought. *Maybe I could still do well in my classes. Maybe I'll go to college. Maybe I'll have a boyfriend one day. Maybe a man will love me enough to ask me to marry him. Maybe I will be somebody. Maybe there is hope.*

7

LIVING EVERY DAY TO THE FULLEST

The last person I ever expected to follow emerged as my leader and became one of my greatest sources of support. She was a classmate, who ironically was someone I had relentlessly teased before falling ill. Her name was Deanne and she was taller than everyone else, stronger than everyone else, and more athletic than everyone else.

You would think that given her athletic abilities, she would be popular. But the mean girls thought she was gay. In the fifth and sixth grade, we persistently mocked her, calling her a "fruiter," our word for a lesbian. She had a short, boy-like haircut with a flat chest and the build of a young man. I don't think she really was gay. But we taunted her because she wasn't like us. She wasn't pretty, or girly, or into boys like the rest of us. She was different and I was a bully.

But now, regardless of her sexual orientation, the truth was that I didn't fit in and she didn't fit in. We were both outcasts. And despite the way I had previously treated her, she was the one person who stood by my side while all my other friends were too embarrassed to hang out with me. We would eat lunch together, she would carry my backpack because I had trouble hauling it on my own, and she was my protector. She was the one who pushed that kid away who tried to knock me out of my wheelchair to prove that I was faking it.

"Leave her alone before I kick your butt," she yelled as she grabbed him by his backpack and flung him across the sidewalk. From that moment on, I thanked God for Deanne, and her friendship meant the world.

When we were fourteen, Deanne started to talk about trying out for the volleyball team.

"I wish I could play volleyball," I said.

"Why not? You can!"

Together, we trained every day during lunch and after school, until I had built up enough strength in my right leg so that I could walk without the leg brace. Not that I didn't need a brace, I still had a significant limp. I just wasn't going to wear an orthotic device as long as I could get around without the discomfort of its plastic edges digging into my foot. Plus, I wanted to do everything I could to be normal, not to be different from my peers. And against the recommendation of my doctors and physical therapist, I stuffed that apparatus in the back of my closet. I was determined never to use it again. I then approached the coach with a limp and dead arm, and told her I wanted to try out for the team.

"Are you sure you want to do this, Michelle?" the volleyball coach asked.

"Yes. I'm no longer in adaptive P.E., I'm taking regular P.E. now because I am getting better. Deanne has been training me. I can do it! I know I can. You have to let me try."

Several months earlier, when I refused to enroll in adaptive P.E. at the start of my freshman year, it caused some issues. Coach Schroeder was all for it. But the regular P.E. teacher, Coach Patterson, was against it.

"You have no place in my P.E. class, Michelle. You are handicapped and I am not going to allow it!" he yelled in front of everyone when I showed up on the first day of class. "You need to go to the office and have them place you in Schroeder's adaptive P.E.," he said pointing in the direction of the administration building. I stood there speechless. "Now go!" he commanded.

I limped away as quickly as I could, completely humiliated. Instead of going to the office, I went to my mom's classroom on the elementary side of the school. She was in the middle of a math lesson with her fourth graders when I burst into her room sobbing hysterically.

"What's wrong?"

"Coach Patterson said I don't belong in his P.E. class because I am handicapped! He said it in front of the entire class. They all laughed at me. It was horrible, Mom! He made me leave the class."

Her mouth dropped. "I will deal with it. Calm down. Why don't you help me with this math lesson? You can stay here until your next class and I will talk to the principal during my recess."

I don't know what my mom told the principal, but Coach Patterson had to apologize to both me and my mom. He said I could stay in his class and that what he said was wrong. I guess that incident got around because none of the coaches were allowed to discriminate against me. That's what my mom told me anyway.

So there I was, trying out for the volleyball team, and no one could stop me. At the informational meeting, the coaches handed out papers to all the athletes explaining requirements and procedures. The first document said that if a player had an injury, the doctor had to write a note stating the date when that player could resume normal physical activities. For me, however, I knew there was no such date. Unlike what the doctors had initially assumed, my condition was permanent. The second page went on to list the activities that the players would be required to do in order to train, each of which required running, or the use of muscles over which I had no control.

After I finished reading the documents, I looked up and scanned the room. There were no words spoken, but I knew what the other girls were thinking; it was written all over their faces.

What is Michelle doing here? Is she going to be able to play? She walks with a limp and can't even run. Doesn't she have a brain tumor or something?

Although I wanted to play so badly, I realized that I couldn't; my body wouldn't permit it. I became angry with myself for getting my hopes up and disappointed in myself for already giving up. I knew that if I tried, I would end up feeling embarrassed, frustrated, and emotionally drained. Who was I kidding?

Yet Deanne was there with me at the meeting. She believed in me and refused to let me quit. My former enemy had become my closest ally. I was so mean to her before I got sick, but now, in my weakest moment, she was my biggest cheerleader, encouraging me every step of the way.

I got my doctor to sign the consent forms and I mustered up the courage to attend spring training tryouts. I expected the other girls to criticize me, but it was just the opposite and they were incredibly supportive. During practice one day I was talking with Karen who was older and from the varsity team. She told me that she admired me for having the guts to try out in the first place. With hours of daily practice, I learned to serve with one hand and I became pretty good at hitting the ball over the net. I would then skip to the place where I thought the ball would be returned and clasped my hands together with the grip of my good hand to bump the ball to another teammate. I still wasn't able to run, but I did my best to move around the area as quickly as I could.

At the end of the tryouts, I waited with the other girls for the results. Daring to hope, but fearing the worst. When the list was finally posted, I quickly scanned down. I saw Deanne's name. I couldn't believe my eyes and blinked as I scanned again. There, toward the bottom of the alphabetical list was typed, "Michelle Taylor."

The year I made the team was the same year the doctors told us that a sizeable portion of the AVM remained implanted in my brain. Another routine MRI revealed that it was inoperable, which we already knew, but that a third radiation treatment would likely compromise my ability to speak or understand language. I knew it was still there, I could feel the *whoosh*, although it had become less persistent, and the doctor made it clear that it wasn't a matter of *if* I would have another bleed, but *when*.

"If untreated, you will be lucky to live to the age of thirty," the doctor said candidly.

When my mom asked what to do next, my neurosurgeon outlined our limited options with the last alternative being, "Just live every day to the fullest." For me, it was about quality of life, not quantity. I was tired of the hospital. I didn't want more treatment. So at the age of fourteen, I vowed to live each day to the fullest.

"Are you sure that's what you want?" my mom asked.

"Yes," I said confidently. "I know this is what I want."

"But the AVM is still there."

"I don't care. I can't go through more treatment and risk becoming more disabled than I already am. I'm not doing it."

It was like I had no more tears left to cry and that decision made me stronger. I was matter of fact about my circumstances, which made me try harder in order to achieve all my goals. I wasn't into all the alternative medicines like I was before either. I no longer had time for that with my school and volleyball schedule. As long as I could focus on school and sports, I would be okay. And I was no longer angry with God. I knew he was there, but I didn't really have a relationship with him. All I knew for sure was that I was tired of being sad. I was tired of being angry. I just wanted to be happy. I wanted to be normal.

In spite of having a significant disability, during my freshman year of high school I played volleyball first string and was the class president. My classmates no longer teased me, but seemed to accept me for who I now was. Maybe it was because of my tenacity in trying out for volleyball that made their opinions change. But what other people thought no longer mattered that much to me; I had moved my sights to bigger and better things. I saw new and beautiful places when I traveled to Hawaii on a family vacation. I slalom water-skied in and out of the wake for the first time since I lost the use of my right side. I was even able to teach myself how to ride a bike again. Deanne had given me that confidence. Not only did she accept me for who I was, but she also showed me what forgiveness looked like at a crucial point in my life when nothing else seemed to make sense.

When I was a sophomore, I was the volleyball junior varsity captain and had a great time being part of a team. That's also the year Deanne moved away. Although I was sad to lose such a great friend, she left me with the gift of self-esteem, giving me the courage to believe in myself under any circumstances.

During my junior year I made the varsity team. I could hardly believe it! I had to repeat it to myself over and over in order to believe it. *Was it a cruel joke?*

I couldn't run, I couldn't overhand serve with one hand, but I tried with all my heart, and I guess that was all that mattered. The fact that I never gave up and that I had the courage to put myself out there—I knew that's what made the difference.

I also knew my life was going to be cut short. But I did my best not to dwell on that. I kept focused on the things I could control.

8

A LESSON IN A CEMETERY

When I was fifteen, one summer day my family went to visit Uncle John, who was my step-dad's brother. I'd always liked him; he was genuine and kind. He'd never married and had no children, so he was always busy doing charity work. He'd built homes for the poor living in Vietnam, reunited a homeless veteran living on the streets of Long Beach with his family in New Jersey, and provided free housing for a single mother working to put her son through college. I loved hearing his stories and I wanted to be like him.

One day, while all my sisters and cousins were playing on the sand in front of his home on Balboa Island, he and I sat on his porch under an old, sprawling rubber tree as he told me about the faraway places he had seen. America, Europe, Asia. I was enchanted by his travel stories, and I longed to create my own.

"I want to go, Uncle John," I said with excitement. "Will you take me? You can take all of us," I said, pointing to the other children building sandcastles on the shoreline. "We should go to Europe!"

"Well, hey, hey, hey," he said, smiling while snapping his right hand and running the other hand through his thick silvery hair. "Yes, dear, I-I-I wi-wi-illl take you some-mum-day." Uncle John had been stuttering since he was a boy and perhaps his speech impediment was one of the reasons I felt so connected to him. He dealt with an obvious limitation every day, but he never let it prevent him from following his dreams or accomplishing his goals. In fact, when he spoke, I didn't hear how he said something, I heard the content of what he said.

Maybe that's how people think of their interactions with me. Maybe they don't even notice that half of my body doesn't work, and instead, focus on my heart, the substance of who I am.

All the same, I never forgot his promise to take us to Europe and knew I would have to remind him each time I saw him until we had our plane tickets in hand.

During the summer of 1999, before the start of my senior year of high school, his promise became reality. He took three of us. My stepsister Chay, my cousin Shana, and I boarded a plane with my uncle at John Wayne Airport in Orange County, headed for Brussels, Belgium. My right leg was in a walking cast, not from the paralysis, but from a fracture I had incurred just a couple weeks prior from walking with a limp without a brace. Still, there was no way I was going to let that stop me. I was used to limping along, so cast or no cast, I was going.

Prior to going to Europe, I had chopped off all my hair. I had beautiful, long, waist length, curly hair, that one day I decided was no longer for me. I wanted a change. I needed to redefine myself. So I went to the hairdresser and told her I wanted a bob, and a bob is what she gave me. My longest strand of hair only measured three inches. In Europe, many of the women had short hair, so I fit right in.

From Belgium we took a train to Amsterdam where we visited Anne Frank's house, also known as the "Secret Annex." There, ten Jews went into hiding after they, like thousands of others, received a notice to "report for work." At that time her "house" was the third floor of a warehouse, with a bookcase that hid the entrance to the Secret Annex.

I carefully opened the bookcase, which swung out on hinges, and walked into the room where Anne Frank and her family struggled to survive while hiding from the Nazis. I already knew most of the story since I'd had to read *The Diary of Anne Frank* in junior high. The Nazis found them, tortured them, and put them in concentration camps where Anne died a month before the camp was liberated.

However, her story suddenly became real when I saw her original diary sitting open on a podium encased in glass. It was opened to April 1, 1944. In German she wrote, "We're hiding, we're Jews in chains without any rights. . . . We must be brave and strong." I looked at the bare, cracked walls that were yellow from age, the walls between which she once lived, and realized that courage is what kept her going.

I learned a great lesson from history that day: that no matter when we live, courage is still a catalyst for change. It inspires and motivates us to persevere when it seems the odds are against us. Anne Frank never stopped dreaming of one day becoming a journalist and she continued to write in spite of the terror happening outside. And even though she never knew it, her work has become one of the most renowned journalist pieces of her time. I thought about my own struggles and realized how small they were compared to the battle Anne faced. Her fight was so intense that she was caught in the middle of a world war, facing religious persecution, hiding from those who wanted her dead. Yet she never gave up, and I vowed not to either.

Overwhelmed with emotion, I walked outside the museum and took a long, deep breath. I looked up and saw that the seagulls flew just the same over the Amsterdam canals as they did over Balboa's bay in California. The clouds hung like white cotton candy with the crisp cool air giving way to a slight breeze. I was suddenly at peace and knew that Anne was too.

The next morning we boarded a train to Henri-Chapelle, a quaint town in the countryside of Belgium about seventy miles southwest of Brussels, known mostly for the American cemetery, where some eight thousand fallen soldiers of World War II rest. Valerie Scudder's brother, Ted Schmidt, died on February 17, 1945. Valerie was my uncle John's and my stepfather Craig's mother. I loved hearing Uncle John tell me stories about his mother.

"In 1960, during a difficult time in her life, my mother wrote a letter to physician and Nobel Peace Prize recipient, Dr. Albert Schweitzer, and asked if she might be permitted to visit him in Africa," my uncle John told me, as he stuttered his way through. "She was never afraid to ask a question, and although she wasn't sure if he would respond, he did, and he said she was welcome. So she packed her suitcase, leaving my father, my three brothers, and me at home, and headed to Lambarene on the Ogooue River. His hospital was in the country of Gabon, located in West Africa, not too far from the equator.

"While she was there, Valerie observed patients arriving daily by pirogue, or canoe, as they paddled in from across the river. Sometimes the natives would also travel by foot, walking a day's journey without any shoes, seeking treatment for everything from leprosy or malaria to more typical medical problems such as a broken limb or a common cold. Regardless of condition, no person was ever turned away.

"She would spend long hours talking with Dr. Schweitzer, learning of his humanitarian efforts, discussing idealism translated to action, and listening to him play the organ. His central belief was 'reverence for life' and felt we are all here to serve others."

Then Uncle John looked at me and smiled. "Life is measured by what we do to serve others."

There I stood in that cemetery, thinking about the kind of person I wanted to become. I knew the cards were stacked against me. After all, I wasn't expected to live past the age of thirty. The doctors had made it clear that with each year, my blood pressure would continue to rise, eventually causing the tangled veins in my brain to burst.

"Your AVM is a ticking time bomb. It's just a matter of time," a doctor once told me.

I knew I could easily give up and wait to die or pursue a life of drugs and alcohol in attempts to cope with my reality. But I knew I was meant for more than that. What my calling was, I had no clue, but I vowed to continue looking until I found it.

There in the fifty-seven acre cemetery in Henri-Chapelle, Uncle John knelt by the grave where Ted Schmidt's name was etched across the top of the stone cross and gently laid a bouquet of calla lilies on his grave, a symbol of holiness, faith, and eternity. We all paid our respects in a moment of silence for his ultimate sacrifice in service to our country.

My uncle wiped a tear from his eye, rose to his feet, and began walking. We trailed behind him like quiet baby chicks following their mother hen until we were back at the train station headed to Bruges.

In a three-week period, we saw seven countries and had the opportunity to spend quality time with our uncle who shared words of wisdom, setting an example for us to follow:

Have good manners. Always over-tip the waitress. Be polite no matter how rudely you are treated. You can lose money, but you can't lose experiences. Have good morals and don't stray from them. You will know when you find "the one." Don't settle. Follow your dreams, no matter what they are. Believe in yourself. Above all, be of service to others as life is filled with endless opportunities to extend a helping hand. And my favorite, don't live your life like a can of refried beans. Meaning, be innovative. Try new things. Step outside of yourself. God gave you a brain, now go and use it.

On the plane ride home, my uncle asked to see my journal. He opened it to the last blank page and started to write.

When he handed it back to me, I flipped it open to that page and read:

Michelle—

What a time we have had. I enjoyed your upbeat spirit and know too, under the circumstances, it wasn't always easy for you moving about Europe. For me, I'm glad to be a part of the memories you will have for a lifetime. As your life begins to unfold in bigger pictures than you have ever known, I wish you so well. . . . You are very dear.

Love, John
10. July. 1999

9

BEYOND MY OWN BACKYARD

After returning from Europe, I went to the doctor, who gave me permission to remove my walking cast. I was changed. My right leg was more atrophied but my mind was more resolute. I knew there was a world out there that extended beyond the realm of Southern California and the experience left me with a hunger to explore and increase my knowledge about the places and people I did not know.

In September, I began my senior year. Again, this year I made the volleyball team, and this time I was voted the varsity volleyball team captain. I was by far the worst player on the team, but I certainly had the greatest team spirit. I was the most enthusiastic bench warmer in our league and my teammates loved me for it! That was also the year I acted as the president of student body, was crowned homecoming queen, and because I kept up with my studies, I was ranked as the salutatorian of my class.

In my gut, I knew that my life would be what I would make it. And in a way, that mindset made me forget about the AVM that still threatened my life with each beat of my heart, which ultimately allowed me to focus on whatever was going on at the time. Volleyball. Planning a school dance. Getting my driver's license. Studying for my AP classes. I had reached a point where I could no longer dwell on the past, but instead, focus on the here and the now, which gave me permission to plan for my future. And my mom was a huge support.

She was adamant that I was going to college. There was never any other choice.

"You need to get a degree, Michelle, since you can't do manual labor."

"Well, I'm not going to be a construction worker!" I laughed.

"I know. But I mean you can't work as a waitress or something like that, because it requires both hands. I put myself through college working as a waitress and believe me, it's hard work."

"I know, Mom."

"So you have to keep up your grades and apply for every scholarship possible. I will help as much as I can, but you need to help me by getting some scholarships. I can't do this alone."

Following high school, I moved into the dorms at California Lutheran University, a small Christian college situated in the foothills of Ventura County, three hours north from home. I wanted to attend a private Christian school, a place where I believed the other students were more likely to accept me. Plus they gave great financial aid, and when combined with the scholarships that I received, I was able to get my first two years of college paid for. Mom took care of the rest.

There, I took a less active social role and instead immersed myself in my studies. I refused to enroll in disability support services and learned to type all my papers with my left hand. The irony of it was that I was paid by the school to be a note taker for people with disabilities through a work study program. It was like the blind leading the blind. But during my sophomore year, it led to Chanelle, a dyslexic student whom I was assigned to take notes for.

We had planned to meet in front of class so that we could introduce ourselves and find a seat next to each other.

"Are you Chanelle?" I asked.

"Yes. Are you Michelle?"

I smiled. "Chanelle and Michelle. That rhymes!"

And we both started laughing hysterically. Chanelle had a huge smile and I found that she giggled a lot, which I loved. She was petite and cute, with shoulder-length, straight brown hair.

"I haven't seen you before. Are you new here?"

"Yeah. I just transferred from Oregon State University. I was in a sorority, but they don't have those here, do they?"

"No. CLU is a dry campus."

"How do you make friends?"

"I don't know. Hanging out in the dorms, I guess. Do you want to hang out?"

"Sure! What dorm are you in?"

"Rasmussen."

"Me too!"

"Awesome. Let me know if you can't read my writing. I had to learn to write with my left hand because I lost the use of my right side after going through radiation for a lesion in my brain."

"Oh no! Are you okay now?"

"The lesion is still there, but I'm fine."

"I got in a car accident when I was seven and broke my neck," Chanelle said. "They said I might never walk again. I used to drool and everything. It wasn't fun."

"Oh my goodness! I'm sorry. You're good now though, right?"

"Yeah. I still drool sometimes, but other than that and my dyslexia, I'm good."

"Well, if you can't read my writing, I will type my notes and can help you study for the tests."

We became instant friends and hung out every day. She had an adventurous spirit like me, and together, we drove into Los Angeles on the weekends to see the Hollywood sign, people-watched on Venice Beach, and if we had enough gas money, we would take a road trip to San Francisco. For my twenty-first birthday, we even went sky diving together. But after just one year at CLU, she transferred to another school closer to home.

Although I missed Chanelle, I knew my adventures would continue in the fall when I would study abroad on a program called Semester at Sea. I wanted to go beyond my own backyard and see not just Europe, but the world. In fact, I did what my mom did thirty years prior and set sail on a ship that took me and seven hundred other students 28,000 miles around the world on a three-month voyage. It was a program that Valerie Scudder, Uncle John's and Craig's mom, started out of Chapman University. She recruited many of the neighborhood kids to attend, including my mother. I had heard about this program all of my life, and it was something my mother insisted that I do.

"Michelle, you have to go on Semester at Sea. It will be the most memorable experience of your life. I'll pay for it, so there are no excuses."

"What's it like?"

"While at sea, you study and earn college credit. While in port, you travel in groups or independently. I would stick to the groups though. It's safer."

I smiled.

"I'm telling you, Michelle. You have to be careful and never get separated from the group."

"I know, Mom. You've told me this a thousand times before."

"Oh, but Michelle, you will love it! You'll see places you couldn't even dream of. And you will realize just how lucky we are to be living in America."

"What do you mean?"

"Everywhere else in the world, there is so much poverty."

"Europe wasn't like that."

"I know. But on this trip you will visit many communist countries where the governments control the people's food, their education, their healthcare, even their salaries. Most people have nothing. They live on less than a dollar a day. This trip will change your life, I guarantee it."

"Cool. I'm excited," I said.

"I just pray that you don't have another bleed while abroad," she said under her breath.

"Mom, I won't. You have to stay positive."

"I know, but it's my job to worry."

"Well, if it does, then it does. But I can't let my AVM prevent me from living. You know that."

"I know. That's why I have given you every opportunity to live out your dreams." She looked away, wiping a tear from her eye.

"All we have is today, Mom. You can't worry about what hasn't happened."

"I know. I love you sweetie pie," she said giving me a hug.

"I love you too."

So with my mom's blessing, I boarded the ship and stood on deck with the other students to wave goodbye to our families. As the ship's crew drew its lines from the dock and the engines propelled us out into the harbor, I saw my mom's figure grow smaller in the distance. We waved goodbye and blew kisses, knowing that medical assistance would be limited if I had another stroke. But I had a life to live, and there was no turning back.

During my three-month voyage I climbed the Great Wall of China. I visited the Taj Mahal in India. I went on safari in Africa. I heard Fidel Castro speak in Cuba. Yet unlike the suburbs of Southern California, I discovered a world where communism prevented people from being free, where Indian children were dying of starvation while cows roamed the streets, where 26 percent of the African population was suffering from AIDS. As the future leaders of our community, our nation, and our world, we learned that we must foster reconciliation and find a common denominator with those who are different from us. We must have a greater vested interest in one another, rather than in our government, the environment, or the world economy.

When I returned to America, although I had come home, I was utterly lost. I had forgotten how to drive a car. I was amazed that I could open my own refrigerator and have cold food at my disposal. The concept of a trash compactor blew my mind. I'd push the pedal at its base and would watch in wonder as it would slide out toward me. I'd close it, push the start button, and listen as the garbage was being smashed to the bottom of the bag. Hot and cold water at the turn of a lever—clean water that was readily available to drink from the faucet without having to boil it first. Grocery stores, shopping malls, specialty shops, where for a price, I could buy anything I wanted. In most of the communist countries I had visited, the government told you what you could buy, what you could eat, and who you would be. The abrupt change affected me so deeply that for two weeks, I locked myself in my room just to get away from all the hustle and bustle. My experience abroad left me in a daze, trying somehow to make sense of the inequality, pain, and suffering that filled our world.

Several weeks later, I sat at my uncle John's kitchen table still feeling overwhelmed—but this time it was not from the third world countries I had seen, but from the reality of being back in a country where our resources seemed inexhaustible. I gave him a box of cigars that I had brought him from Cuba, which thrilled him; he poured us a glass of wine, and said, "You're twenty-one now, aren't you?"

"In two months I will be."

"Close enough," he said as he filled my glass with Toasted Head, his favorite chardonnay.

Not one for small talk, we cut to the heart of things. I paused, rubbed the stem of my wine glass between my fingers and my thumb, and said, "We live in a place where food can be preserved in a refrigerator for weeks. Where we can get in our car and go anywhere we want, whenever we want. Where real education and life-saving health-care are at our fingertips. Where we're given the freedom of speech, to express our thoughts and our feelings as we please."

I sniffled as tears streamed down my face. Uncle John pushed a box of tissue toward me and took one for himself.

"I just don't know what to do. I don't know how to process every-thing," I said before blowing my nose. "Even though I know God has a plan for me, a part of me always felt that I had been cheated before I took this trip. Now I feel incredibly blessed." My uncle reached his hand across the table, clasped mine, and although he was crying also, he smiled and said, "This is only the beginning, dear. This is only the beginning."

10

MY NURSING HOME ROMANCE

During my first semester of my senior year I took a class called "Death & Dying." While I was intrigued by the topic, what really caught my attention was a handsome, six foot, slender, blue-eyed, blond-haired student who had a *real* job outside of school. His name was Steven. And unlike the other boys, he had manners, always opening the classroom door for the girls and letting them go in before him. Although I was impressed by him, I was too shy ever to talk to him. It didn't help that during class debates, he sat on the conservative side of the room and I was with all the liberals.

We are worlds apart, I thought. Still, there was something about him, and I would often catch myself gazing at him across the room.

Even though I was intrigued with this man, there was still school-work to be done. As part of a class assignment, each student had to volunteer at a nursing facility and write a biography about a resident's life. After being randomly assigned, I met my eighty-four year old patient, Betsy, who was permanently placed in the facility because she, coincidentally, had suffered a massive stroke.

Due to left side paralysis, Betsy had difficulty speaking and was initially embarrassed to try—until I shared with her that I had also experienced a stroke, and like her, half of my body was paralyzed. We developed an immediate bond, one that transcended age and time. From then on I would visit Betsy every Tuesday at 4:00 p.m. for one hour.

After several visits, she told me about the new clock on her wall. "I had the staff put a clock up for me so that I know when you are coming," she managed to say, pointing to it with her good hand. Being completely bed bound, she now had something to look forward to, and I never missed a visit.

During our time together I learned that Betsy was a life-long educator. She was a woman who had earned her master's degree by the age of twenty-three in the 1930s, passionately pursuing her dream of becoming a school teacher. She later married the superintendent of a school district and they were blessed with four children.

One day as we were talking about life, I asked her what thing she loved to do the most. With slurred speech she said, "I used to love to read, but I can't anymore because the stroke affected my vision." On my next visit I brought a book of short biographies about great American women and I read a chapter to her every week until the week she died.

The next time class met, the professor announced that two students had made such an impact on their patient's lives that the families had asked both of them to give the eulogy at their loved one's funeral.

"The students are Michelle and Steven," the professor announced.

I looked around the room until our eyes met. We both smiled, my heart fluttered, and I felt the blood moving up through my neck, into my cheeks and ears. I'm sure my face turned bright red. It turned out that Steven's patient had passed away two days after Betsy.

Later that night, the class attended the Christmas party at the nursing facility, and because both of our patients were no longer there, Steven sat by me.

"Is this seat taken?" he asked.

"No," I said with a childlike grin pasted across my face.

"Wow. Can you believe we were both asked to give the eulogy for our patients?"

"No, I really can't. I am so honored. My patient barely even knew me."

"Yeah. It is quite an honor. You must have made an impact on her. What are you going to say at the funeral?"

"I think I'm going to read excerpts from Betsy's biography, have a copy ready for each of her children, and tell them all of the stories that she was able to share with me. Like how her dormitory burned down to the ground during her freshman year of college and how the car salesman taught her to drive *after* she bought her first car."

"Really?"

I nodded. "I'll talk about how even though she was busy raising four children, she still managed to volunteer her time. When I asked her what motivated her to help, she said, 'I just believe the world has given me so much that I owed something back.' She told me, 'There is not enough love in this world. Too much me-first, and no one ever worries about anyone else. Yet even in spite of life's unpleasantries, there are still more good people than there are bad.' I agree with her. Don't you?"

Steven leaned in closer. In a softer tone, he replied, "Yeah, I've spent a lot of time volunteering. I recently helped my church build a house for teenage pregnant women."

"Really? I work at the Women's Resource Center on campus. You should stop by sometime and check it out." I felt my palms sweating and I just couldn't stop smiling.

"I will."

"What are you going to say at Earl's funeral?"

"I have no idea," he said with a nervous laugh. "I'll have to think about that one."

It was time for us to leave, so Steven walked me to my car. I wondered if he noticed my limp on the way out.

Will he care? I wondered uneasily. *Will he like me after I tell him what's wrong with me? He must have already noticed from seeing me in class. Or maybe he just never paid attention. He seems so different from the other guys; maybe it won't matter to him.*

We stood by my silver Volkswagen Jetta gazing into each other's eyes, and a crazy thought flitted into my mind: *I'm going to marry this man.*

All of my doubts disappeared in a vision. I saw that he had a sister and I knew exactly what she looked like. Blond, petite, and bubbly. I saw Steven and me on our wedding day. I saw the gown I would wear and the tux he had on. I saw the water—we would be married by the ocean—and I saw the stained glass window of the church. True to

Uncle John's word, I knew that Steven was "the one" and that through our patients' deaths, God had brought us together.

I snapped back to reality, we said our goodbyes, and I floated home, feeling an excitement I'd never felt before.

At Betsy's funeral I stood at the podium, twenty-one years old, talking about a woman whom I had known for only two months, sharing the story of her life and the motto she lived by, "Just enjoy life. Accept things as they are. Hope for the best, but take whatever comes."

Afterward, one of her sons told me, "You said things I never knew about my mother, because I never took the time to ask."

His words made me sad. "She loved you very much. She was a really wonderful lady," I said reaching out to touch his arm.

All it took was an hour of my time, once a week, to really make a difference, I thought.

The following week Steven waited for me after class and walked me home. I had to find a way to tell him what was wrong with me. I couldn't stop thinking about it since I started falling for him at the skilled nursing facility. All I could think about was something a guy I had dated had once told me: "You know, you are really lucky to have me. Not many guys would ever go for you because of what's wrong with you." Those words had haunted me for years. I had lived it. I had met a lot of guys who were initially interested—until I told them that I was permanently disabled because of a stroke and that I still had an inoperable brain lesion, ready to explode at any minute without warning. Then suddenly they weren't interested in me any longer.

The knots were tightening in my stomach and I could feel my anxiety growing more intense with each second. Would Steven reject me or would he accept me? I couldn't stand it any longer. He was talking but I wasn't listening to a word he was saying.

I blurted out, "I don't know if you've noticed, but my right side is paralyzed. I had a stroke when I was eleven and that's when they discovered that I had an Arteriovenous Malformation in my brain, an AVM. It's a tangle of blood vessels and arteries in my brain that cause hemorrhagic strokes. I went through two radiation treatments, but the remainder is inoperable. It's really no big deal though. I'm completely normal. I am very determined and can still do everything a regular person does." In my mind, I was pleading with him, *Please like me anyway. Please don't care. Please!*

Without skipping a beat, he said, "Wow. I'm sorry. My aunt is a little person and she can't walk without crutches. I grew up near her, so I'm used to things like that."

"It doesn't bother you?"

"Not at all. Why would it?"

"It just seemed to bother other guys in the past."

"Well, I'm not other guys."

I smiled. "I know, you're better." I still couldn't believe it though.

We arrived at my front door and he pulled a card out of the pocket of his leather jacket.

"This is for you."

"What is it?"

"It's a card. But don't open it until I leave."

I was doing flips and cartwheels on the inside; my cheeks hurt from smiling.

"Okay."

"I have to go, but I'll call you."

He hugged me goodbye and I went inside, closed the door, and screamed, "I have a card!" All seven of my roommates came running. They gathered around me as I opened the card. The front cover showed two pink flowers entwined.

"Awe!" we all exclaimed in unison. I opened the card and read it aloud.

Michelle,

In the short time that I have had the chance to talk to you, I can really see how much of an amazing person you are. I admire you and the things that you have accomplished. You have such a compassionate heart and a wonderful outlook on life. You might not realize this, but you are an inspiration and a positive influence in people's lives, especially mine.

Thank you,
Steven

"He loves you, Michelle," Liz squealed!

"You think so?"

"I know so!"

Annika, another roommate chimed in, chanting, "Michelle's got a boyfriend! Michelle's got a boyfriend!"

"No! He doesn't love me. He doesn't even know me. He's just a really nice guy. He probably gives cards like these to all the girls." I was trying to convince myself that it was no big deal in case things didn't work out.

"Michelle, how could you think that? Girls don't get cards like that from guys and he is not the flirtatious type. I promise you, he really likes you," another roommate, Adrienne, insisted.

"What do you think I should do?"

"Has he asked you on a date?" Liz asked.

"Well, we were planning to go to dinner with Frances and Omar, the holocaust survivors. I know them through the Women's Resource Center and Steven once took a class with Frances, but we are having trouble coordinating dates."

"Does he have your number?" Adrienne asked.

"Yes."

"Why don't you call him?" Liz asked.

"Because he said he would call me."

"Well, you will just have to wait then," Annika said, smiling and lifting her eyebrows. "But I don't think you'll be waiting long."

The next day my cell phone rang.

"Hi, Michelle. It's Steven."

"Hi! How are you?"

"Good. Good."

"I just wanted to thank you for the card yesterday. It was very thoughtful."

"No problem. Hey, I wanted to let you know that Frances and Omar can't make it with us to dinner."

My heart sank. "Oh bummer."

"But I was wondering if you still want to go to dinner with me?"

"You mean just me and you?"

"Yes."

"So just the two of us?"

"Yes. Is that okay?"

"Yeah, it's great!"

"Can I pick you up on Friday at five?"

"Yes. That sounds perfect!"

"Okay. See you then."

I started screaming the minute I hung up the phone and ran downstairs to the living room where Liz and Adrienne were doing their homework.

"What happened?" Adrienne asked with a smile.

"I think I have a date!" I went on to tell them what had happened.

"Michelle, it's totally a date!" Liz exclaimed.

"What should I wear?"

"Where is he taking you?" Liz asked.

"I have no idea. He didn't say and I didn't think to ask."

"Don't go too fancy," Adrienne advised. "Remember that one guy who took you on a date to McDonalds? You were way overdressed for that one!"

"That guy was such a loser!" I muttered. "I think Steven has a little more class. Maybe I will wear nice jeans and a black top."

"I think that sounds prefect," Liz said as she stood up to give me a giant hug. "I am so happy for you!"

On our first date, Steven brought me a bouquet of flowers that was so large, they could barely fit through the front door. Over that final semester of college, he wrote me love notes, brought me chocolates, took me to dinner, and even made me soup when I was sick. I kept wanting to pinch myself to wake me from this dream. I couldn't believe that he knew my medical history, he knew about my right arm, Fred, and he accepted all of it. He told me, "It just makes you all the more wonderful."

The thing I was most insecure about was the thing Steven loved the most. He said it was what made me, me.

Within weeks, I fell so hard that he made every other guy I'd ever dated seem insignificant. He was every prayer answered—mine, my mother's, and my grandmother's. Was it too good to be true? Being disabled, I always saw myself as incomplete and thought no guy would ever want to care for me if I had another stroke. There was no doubt, I was a risky investment. Yet here was this man who treated me with love and respect. I knew I had only God to thank.

11

FINDING PURPOSE

One week before we graduated from college, Steven took me to a restaurant in Topanga Canyon where he reserved a private gazebo. In fact, it was so private that the waitress forgot about us. But that didn't matter. We were together.

"There is no one like you, Michelle. I love you so much and I want to spend the rest of my life with you. Will you marry me?" he asked as he pulled out a ring. It was my grandparent's wedding ring that he had gotten from my mother. He had made it our own by adding a band of diamonds to each side.

"Of course! Yes. Yes. Yes!"

There have been moments when I've clearly felt the hand of God on my back, moving me to the exact place I need to be. I felt it when I tried out for the volleyball team in high school. I experienced it when I traveled around the globe on a ship, visiting third world countries. And I sensed it again while I volunteered to work with Betsy in the nursing facility. The moment I said yes to Steven's proposal I knew it was one of those "God" moments. I was finally beginning to understand what it meant to trust God fully with all of my heart.

The summer after we graduated, I found a job that I fell in love with and knew I could spend the rest of my life doing: hospice work. Again, I felt God's hand leading me to it all along. Hospice is a type of care designed to support terminally ill children and adults diagnosed with six months or less to live. A physician, nurse, social worker, chaplain, certified home health aide, and a trained volunteer surround each patient with a community of support intended to address the physical, emotional, and spiritual needs of the dying.

I began my work as a volunteer coordinator. I was responsible for recruiting, training, and retaining volunteers to provide hospice patients with emotional support and companionship. Through my interactions with staff, I then became involved with coordinating the fulfillment of the dying patients' wishes, and I loved it.

When some people would find out about my job they would say, "How can you work for hospice? It must be so depressing." But I felt quite the opposite. I was able to bring a sense of peace to those who only had a short time left on earth. Essentially, when all medical resources have been exhausted, hospice works to transform the traditional standard of hope for a cure, to hope for quality of life, comfort, and dignity with death. Hospice offers an opportunity to change the way people live while they are dying. It is powerful, profound, and exceptionally compassionate.

As I was settling in to my new career, I was also juggling wedding planning, and on April 2, 2005, Steven and I were married. Betsy and Earl left this life, and in doing so brought our lives together. Two souls were taken home and our souls were united as we made the commitment to go before God in holy matrimony.

For our wedding day I wrote Steven a letter:

Steven,

You are the sun that gives me light, the joy that brings me laughter, the shelter that gives me warmth. You are everything that is good, everything that's pure, everything that's true. You are my everything. My one true love. May God bless you always and keep you safe.

With sincere love,
Michelle

And that vision I had when I saw my wedding day and the beach and the stained glass?

It was all true. Who but God could fulfill my every dream?

12

A LEADER IN THE MAKING

The day after our wedding, we closed escrow on our first home, a two-story townhouse in Santa Ana Heights, located in Orange County, California. Aside from new paint and new carpet, it was move-in ready.

Life was good. I had my career, we had our home. Still, I wanted more. I yearned for knowledge. So in 2006, I began studies at Chapman University to pursue a master's degree in organizational leadership, a program geared toward working adults. Armed with my undergraduate degree in psychology, I now wanted to focus on something more business related, while still maintaining a focus on the human element. Ultimately, I wanted to know the secret to creating a great company. Not so that I could make a lot of money, but so that I could make a difference. I was curious about what motivates employees or volunteers to do a wonderful job. What creates an effective team? I wanted to learn how great leaders lead, so I could become a leader in my industry.

I loved every minute of my master's program. I loved that I could apply what I was learning to my job, and like a mad scientist, I tested every leadership theory I learned.

It especially came in handy during one tougher season at my job. Our hospice volunteers seemed to be quitting left and right and I had a growing number of patients whose needs were not being met. I kept asking myself, *What am I doing wrong?* Here I was earning a degree in leadership and yet I was having a difficult time retaining my hospice volunteers.

Their reasons for leaving were legitimate, ranging from starting a new job, an internship had ended, their mother was sick. Before I started graduate school, it seemed that when one volunteer left, another would begin. Things always mysteriously worked out.

But after a failed volunteer recruitment event, where I was unsuccessful in getting anyone to sign up, I sat behind my computer feeling stressed and wondering what I was missing.

Thinking about my leadership classes, I thought, *Am I not effectively modeling behavior? Am I creating an uninviting office culture? Have I created an "in group" and an "out group," and therefore excluded certain individuals?* None of these questions offered valid answers.

And then I realized that prior to my leadership studies, with every success, I had given the credit for that success to God. Since beginning my master's program, instead of attributing my leadership abilities to God's work, I had been attributing them to my own intellectual talent. Consequently, my volunteer program was falling apart.

I realized then that my leadership abilities *are* truly the work of God and that when I stray from that conviction, I begin to falter. When I forget to give him thanks or begin to think that I can do things alone, I fail. No matter how hard I try, I fail. My truest wish was that the Lord would use me for whatever good he intended. My role in leadership was all because of him. I remembered what someone once told me, "The highest place you can seek counsel is on your knees."

And on my knees I went. I pushed back from my computer, knelt by my desk, and prayed,

> *Dear God,*
>
> *Please use me to do your good works. Whatever you want me to be, wherever you want me to go, take me there. Lord, give me the strength and the courage to live out what you have planned. Help guide me when I begin to wander, encourage me when I begin to doubt, and nourish me when I grow weak. Thank you for all the blessings you have given me. Thank you for keeping me safe, and thank you for filling my life with love. Amen.*

As I got back off my knees, I remembered what it meant to live out my best life. I knew that my struggles with the volunteers—in fact, with everything in my life that went awry—was because I had lost sight of what was important and that I was failing to act in alignment with my true purpose.

Suddenly, the issues with my hospice volunteers seemed to fade away. That's what happens when you relinquish power. When you accept that God is in control and you are not, everything *always* works itself out.

13

AND THE RAIN CAME DOWN

As much as we loved our little townhome, we were aching for land. So we purchased our dream home in the neighborhood of Bayview Heights in Newport Beach, California, during the spring of 2007. The house looked the same as it did when it was built in the 1950s: 1,100 square foot, single story, three bedroom, one bathroom with pink tile! My husband was familiar with construction, so he was excited to make this house our home. For three months over the summer, we spent evenings and weekends remodeling until September when we were ready to move in.

We loved our neighborhood and I was reminded of the place where I grew up. A touch of country in the middle of a city with people horseback riding down the streets. Rabbits, chickens, coyotes, bobcats, and other wildlife freely roamed the trails of Newport Beach's back bay. Dog walkers, runners, and mountain bikers were always out and about, enjoying their daily exercise.

It was a wonderful place to live and on top of that, I had pursued my passion for hospice and was now the executive director to a small hospice foundation. I had everything I had ever wanted. My life seemed perfect.

On Friday, January 4, 2008, I spent the day at work as usual. But my master's thesis was nagging at the back of my mind. Although it wasn't due for another week, I knew in my gut that I had to finish it that night. I went home and typed up the last few pages at about six o'clock, transferred the Word document to my thumb drive, hopped in my white Toyota Highlander in the pouring rain, and headed to Kinkos.

At Kinkos I asked an associate to help me get set up at a printer. Suddenly I began to feel ill. I followed the employee to one of the machines, and as I was walking, the room began to spin—as if I had been drinking too much—and it felt as though I might spin up and out of my body. I paused and refocused, but I knew something was terribly wrong. I tried to pull myself together and began printing and binding copies of my thesis.

Finally, I was able to get everything completed. I went to the cashier, and was greeted by a young, slightly overweight woman with long, brown, frizzy hair. She was tearful and I wondered why. I figured it out when the store manager stormed in from behind closed doors, reprimanding her for a mistake she had made. He must have been a few years older than me and clearly knew nothing about management or leadership. As he stood behind her yelling, she took my credit card, and continued apologizing to both me and him, looking neither of us in the eye.

"I'm sorry. I'm so sorry."

I looked at her, looked at him, shook my head, and walked out.

What kind of leader am I not to say anything? But I knew I had to get out of there before I passed out. With the rain still coming down, I stood under the awning waiting for it to let up a little so I wouldn't soak my treasured thesis. I still felt woozy, so I looked at Hoag Hospital, which I could see about a mile away.

Should I go to Hoag, or should I go home?

I figured I was just tired and drove home. The rain pounded against my window and it reminded me of the pounding in my head fourteen years ago when I had my stroke. This moment, though, there was no *whoosh*. There was no headache. I just felt dizzy.

I'm fine. I'm just tired from working and going to school full time. I'll be fine. I just need rest.

I pulled into my driveway. Steven greeted me at the door and asked me how it was.

"The manager at Kinkos was awful," I said. "I have to call their headquarters and file a complaint."

I turned on our computer, looked up the number to Kinkos' customer service department, got on the phone, and reported what had happened. I explained how I was printing my personal philosophy of leadership for my master's program and I couldn't live with myself without saying something. The manager was misusing his power to make a subordinate feel small, humiliating her in front of the customers.

"The manager's behavior was completely uncalled for, and not only was the ordeal embarrassing for her, but it made the customers extremely uncomfortable. You should really have your managers take classes so they can learn how to become better leaders," I said.

The customer service representative assured me that my complaint would be addressed and thanked me for calling. I hung up the phone, walked to the couch, and sat down, falling back into the cushions. Steven noticed that I didn't look right.

"Are you feeling okay?"

"No."

"Do you want some Tylenol?"

"Yes," I whispered.

He gave me two Tylenol and a bottle of water. I put the pills in my mouth, took a swig, and began to lose consciousness.

"What's wrong? Michelle? Michelle!"

I opened my eyes.

"Do you want me to take you to the hospital?"

"Yes." I could only whisper.

"Can you make it to the car?"

"Yes."

Steven jumped into action, grabbed the car keys and my purse, and helped me to my car. I got into the passenger seat and closed my eyes. Steven hopped in the driver's side and started the engine. We drove to the corner of Mesa and Birch Streets, where the light is always red.

"How bad is it?" Steve asked.

"It's not good," I whispered.

"Do you want me to run the red light?"

"Yes."

Steve checked both directions, then hit the gas, and pulled into the fire station across the street, which had just been opened three months prior. He ran to the main entrance of the firehouse. I attempted to follow him, only getting as far as opening my car door when he yelled, "Stay there!"

He pounded on the front door and yelled, "Help! I think my wife is having a stroke! Help!"

The fire captain opened the door and looked at Steven bewildered. "My wife has an AVM. I think she's having a stroke."

The firemen swiftly went into action. They called an ambulance from another station while their paramedic immediately put me on oxygen. I tried to breathe normally as I lay slumped back in my car.

I heard him tell Steven that they needed to keep me conscious.

"Michelle, I'm going to ask you some yes and no questions. Just nod up and down or shake your head from side to side with the answers, okay?" the paramedic told me.

I slowly nodded.

As he began to question me, Steven gave the fire captain my medical history. I felt terrible that they were standing out in the rain getting drenched.

"She was diagnosed with an AVM in December 1993. They found it because she had a stroke. She was only eleven. She had two radiation treatments. The first treatment paralyzed her right side because it zapped the motor strip on the left side of her brain. The rest of the AVM was inoperable." He paused and looked at me. "I knew this day would come, I just didn't think it would happen so soon."

The fire captain asked something and Steven replied, "She's twenty-five. We've been married for two and a half years."

This can't be happening, I thought. *Not again. Not now. There is too much life left for us to live.*

The ambulance arrived ten minutes later and I was swiftly moved onto a bright yellow stretcher. I opened my eyes and saw the gray ceiling of the ambulance, an IV pole, and the face of a paramedic who sat over me, holding both of my shoulders and saying, "Stay with me, Michelle. Michelle, stay with me."

I wanted to obey. I tried. But the last thing I thought before I drifted into blackness was, *I can't hold on anymore. This is it. I have to go.*

14

COMING TO TERMS

At the hospital, the emergency room staff found that I was comatose with right sided posturing, or stiffening of the extremities, a sign of severe brain damage. That also indicated a poor prognosis. My left pupil was blown, enlarged, fixed, and dilated.

Hanging in the balance between life and death, a team of physicians and nurses immediately began cutting off my clothes, inserting IVs, and initiating life support before wheeling me off to receive a CT scan. I had suffered an acute intracranial hemorrhage—a catastrophic stroke.

The ER doctor told my husband, "If we don't surgically remove the AVM, she won't make it through the night, and if we do, she has a 50/50 chance of surviving. Surgery is our only hope." With no other options, my husband signed the consents. Once the on-call neurosurgeon, Dr. Dobkin, arrived, and after my husband prayed over me, the staff wheeled me—intubated and unconscious—into the operating room.

The moment for which the doctors had been preparing us for more than a decade had arrived. My AVM had finally won. In the waiting room, Steven called my mom and stepfather, Craig. My mom went into such a hysterical state that Craig had to call my sisters Ashley, Chay, and Jenna, and my best friend, Christy, to let them know what had happened.

Steven continued to call his family and friends and before long, more than twenty people were gathered in the hospital waiting room, praying, crying, and worrying. They all knew what the doctors had told me for most of my life: there was no way I would survive the surgery without becoming both physically and mentally incapacitated.

Meanwhile, in the operating room, a nurse shaved my head completely, collecting my blonde hair in a red surgical bag, and put it aside. She then carefully placed my head in a Mayfield headrest, a surgical device that provides cranial support during brain surgery, allowing my head to be flexed forward 30 degrees and completely immobilized. With a surgical pen, Dr. Dobkin drew the incision lines on the left side of my head, extending from my motor strip to the posterior parietal region, or the area near the top left back side of my head, the area of the brain controlling right sided movement as well as language and speech.

His team then cleaned the surgical site, began a blood transfusion, made the incision, and removed the skull bone. At that point, a blood clot was removed. Dr. Dobkin then took a scissor-like instrument and attacked the bleeding Arteriovenous Malformation by cutting off the veins that fed it, which caused it to collapse entirely, deflating it like a popped balloon. The total AVM was then removed and sent for analysis.

Next, they inserted a drain tube to continue removing the stroke blood from the left lateral ventricle, a space in the brain that normally contains the cerebrospinal fluid. Finally, the surgeon replaced my skull bone with multiple titanium plates, which he secured with nineteen screws, piecing my skull back together like an intricately complicated, yet delicate puzzle. He stitched closed my skin and wrapped my head in nylon.

As an organ donor, I was a viable candidate for organ donation. On the Glasgow Coma Scale, a fifteen-point scale estimating and categorizing the outcomes of brain injury on the basis of overall social capability or dependence on others, I was rated a three. Donate Life is only contacted when an organ donor is faced with imminent death with a Glasgow Coma Scale rating of five or less. At level three, I was considered to be in a vegetative state and my prognosis was extremely poor.

Nearly six hours after being wheeled into the operating room, I was moved into a recovery area, and Dr. Dobkin went to the waiting room to give my family the update. It was two thirty in the morning.

"The hematoma was quite large, but we were able to remove it along with the AVM," he said.

My mom got straight to the point, "Is she going to make it?"

"The chances aren't good. She only has brainstem activity and evidence of posturing, or involuntary extension of the arms and legs, indicating severe brain injury. If she makes it, she won't be able to walk again. She will have vision problems for the rest of her life and most likely won't be able to talk. Her prognosis is very poor, but we'll just have to wait and see." [1]

---

1   Thanks to my husband, my family, my friends, and my medical records, I've included the details of what happened while I was unconscious.

15

THE PLACE OF PRAYERS

Somewhere caught between life and death, I was no longer of my flesh. I didn't go toward the light, I was the light, and it was all around me. I experienced complete tranquility, an overwhelming, awe-inspiring sense of peace that was unmatched to anything I had ever felt. I was completely enveloped by the presence of God, surrounded by pure love. Like a newborn who is swaddled in its mother's blanket, I was shrouded in a warm cloak of serenity and adoration.

The light itself was soft and calming, giving me remarkable comfort, soothing every part of my being. I didn't need to acclimate to the light because it was as if I had always been a part of it, and a feeling of homecoming overcame my soul. This is where I had come from and this is where now I belonged.

There were no physical forms. There were no people as we know them, only spirits. And despite what one might expect, there was no separation between this spirit and that spirit, my spirit and their spirit. We were all one. An energy force that was mighty and powerful. But the words, *mighty* and *powerful* are not words that convey the message of purity and lovingness that we were. In that place there was no room for pain, no room for suffering. There was no room for evil or wrong doing. All the bad that we know in this world simply did not exist. And there was no sense of time. I could have been there for a minute or for a millennium, allowing me to dwell there for all eternity.

I began to hear voices all around me speaking in every language. Somehow I knew they were the prayers of people around the world rising up to God. I could literally feel the prayers spoken from the lips of my loved ones, and they covered me. Every plea, every request, every hope, and every wish for healing, for a miracle—the prayers surrounded me like the afternoon glow of the setting sun or warm cotton sheets fresh from the dryer, giving comfort I had never known.

"Heal her, Lord God. Let her be healed! We exalt you and we praise your name."

The prayers became louder and more passionate, penetrating every piece of who I was.

"In the name of Jesus, let her be healed!"

Many of the prayers were spoken in tongues, the language of the Holy Spirit, and with each prayer, I could feel the healing begin to take place. Like a laser, the prayers became so concentrated that they shot through me, infusing more light and more peace, lifting me higher and higher. Wrapped in everything that is beautiful, everything that is good, I understood God's perfect love. It was like a synchronization so salient, it was more melodious than the finest orchestra in all the world. A song so divine that I was swept away and cradled in the gentle arms of angels. There was no doubt: I was with God and God was with me, and together, we were one.

After several hours the staff moved me to the neurological intensive care unit and began to wean me off the sedations to monitor my neurological status for improvements. The doctors recommended that I have as little stimulation as possible to allow my brain to heal. As a result, Steven decided that no one could visit me except for my parents and his parents. He wanted to follow the doctor's orders and do everything he could to create a healing environment.

Steven stayed by my side, sleeping on a tiny cot placed next to my hospital bed. He prayed, held my hand, and read my thesis aloud over and over.

I survived the night, but on the second day I still showed no improvements. Knowing how important it was to me to pass my class, Steven called Tammara and Mary, two of my closest friends from graduate school, arranged for them to pick up my thesis from the hospital, and turn it in on our last day of class.

By this point word had spread about my impending death. My dad drove from Arizona, and my friend Chanelle, who was eight months pregnant, along with her husband, Ian, jumped on a plane from San Francisco to Orange County, wearing pajamas and flip flops.

As more people arrived, they were all asked to remain in the waiting room, since Steven's mind was made up. He wanted my brain to heal and he refused to let anyone cry at my bedside. He made it clear to the family and the hospital staff that he did not believe I was going to die. Whenever a nurse or physician asked Steven to complete an advanced directive, a document that states your wishes in regards to life-sustaining measures, he would crumble it in his hands and throw the document in the trash.

By day three, I was still unconscious. Steven brought his laptop to work at the hospital, and continued to sleep at my bedside. On top of my medical condition, Steven had recently learned that his job at Starbucks was uncertain. The company was downsizing and he was faced with the possibility of losing his job and our health insurance.

On day four, my family started an interactive blog on a website called Caringbridge.com where my family could post updates and people could respond to the posts, similar to Facebook or MySpace. On Tuesday, January 8, 2008, my mom wrote:

> *My Michelle!*
> *"Live life to the fullest because we don't know what tomor-row will bring." Your doctor told you that some years ago and that is just what you have been doing. I have never known some-one with so much drive and ambition. You always knew that your time would be short and you wanted to get all of your goals accomplished. You are such an angel. You have touched so many lives. You have been so concerned lately about my care when I get*

old. Everyone is praying for you, my Michelle. You already know how much I love you.

My sister Ashley wrote:

My beautiful sister:
I love you so much. Not a day has gone by that I haven't been here at the hospital. I will continue to be here until you wake up and I can see that beautiful face, that precious smile. I will live the rest of my life in honor of you. I promise you and God that I will make a mark on this earth because of you. You mean the world to me and I can't wait for you to come home. You are the strongest individual I have ever met and I know that this will just give you more strength and determination to conquer the world! I love you with all of my heart and soul!

On day five, I began gagging on the breathing tube and the nurses had to subdue me with more medications to prevent me from displacing life support.

As Steven watched my movement, he became more adamant that everything would be okay. The physicians, however, continued to disagree. They told Steven that neurologically, I had sustained a catastrophic brain hemorrhage and that the overall prognosis for meaningful recovery remained poor, considering the lack of neurological improvement over the last five days.

When someone is in a coma, many people debate whether or not that person can hear.

I could hear everything.

I could hear people asking me to open my eyes or to squeeze their hand if I could hear them. I tried opening my eyes, I tried squeezing their hand, but I was so weak, I didn't have the strength to follow their commands. The weight of my eyelids were so heavy, they felt as if they were made of thick steel. No matter how hard I tried, my fingers simply wouldn't move. I wasn't frustrated though. I wasn't trapped in my body as one might expect. I was at peace.

At this point, I was drifting in and out of the *Place of Prayers.* A part of me didn't want to come back. How could I return to a broken world after being with God? How could I leave such a beautiful place where I was surrounded by complete love? But I could hear the desperate prayers of my loved ones, asking for a miracle. They wanted me back and many praised God as if it had already happened. My hesitation to leave God's holy presence became determination when I heard the Lord say, "But I am with you always," and I knew it was so.

16

FAITH, HOPE, HEALING

Steven's father, Rick, a pastor for more than thirty years with Foursquare Church International, was a part of the corporate leadership team working with Pastor Jack Hayford. They were lifting many concentrated prayers up to God on my behalf, asking for complete restoration and healing. Also many friends and family, including people from Mariners, our home church, were praying, and I could feel the love that was being poured over me.

In spite of this, however, I continued to be nonreactive to any stimuli, remaining in a vegetative state. Since I could still hear, though, I had a pretty good sense of what I must have looked like. I overheard someone make a comment about all the tubes covering me—as though I looked half human and half machine. My scalp felt wrapped in a dressing that had some sort of drain tube protruding from the center of my head, my mouth and throat were stuffed with a breathing tube, a feeding tube went through my nose, and IVs were stuck in my arms. I couldn't have moved even if I had been able to.

While Steven went home to shower in the evenings, my mom would stay with me. On that fifth night, she began reading all the get well cards to me that had been sent by family and friends. As she continued to read, the kindness of everyone who cared about me overwhelmed my heart. A tear streamed down my left check. My mom started screaming, "Oh my goodness, she can hear me! She can hear me!"

A nurse ran into the room.

"I was reading her all these get well cards and a tear rolled down her face! She can hear me! She is still here!" my mom exclaimed.

"She is probably just in pain," the nurse responded. "I will give her more medicine."

The next morning, day six, the doctor had a conversation with Steven in my room. The doctor's assessment was that my long-term prognosis was poor, that I would likely be dependent upon a vent for some time, and would require a tracheotomy for airway protection as well as a gastrostomy tube for feeding.

"The sooner we can insert those, the better," the doctor said.

"I understand what you're saying, but I'd like to delay the procedure for as long as possible in case she does wake up."

"Well, today's Thursday, but unfortunately, we have to schedule the procedure for tomorrow. Leaving the breathing tube in for more than seven days can cause permanent damage."

"I wish we could wait," Steven replied.

"I'm sorry but we really don't have too many options at this point."

Later an elderly lady from housekeeping entered the room to change the trashcan. In broken English she asked Steven what my name was.

"Michelle Gwen Wulfestieg," he told her. "She is strong and she is going to pull out of this setback."

"I pray for her tonight. I keep praying. God bless you. I pray, okay?"

Believe it or not, I heard her prayers. She spoke the Lord's Prayer, and although I don't speak Spanish, I heard and understood every word as they resounded through my entire being.

And at the conclusion of the prayer, the Lord said, "You must return to tell the world of my glory."

On day seven I was able to briefly open my eyes and look around the room. As soon as I opened them, however, the weight of my eyelids overwhelmed me and I quickly closed them again, and I faded back into my now normal state of unresponsiveness.

"Michelle? Michelle! I'm right here. Can you see me?" I heard Steven's voice rise with excitement. But I just couldn't respond.

He gripped my hand. I could hear desperation mingle with the excitement in his voice now. "Michelle! I love you. Can you hear me? Can you open your eyes? Michelle, I love you."

After a few moments, he began to pray:

Dear God,
   Thank you so much for allowing Michelle to open her eyes. Thank you for healing her body. Please, please continue to heal her body. Continue to restore her back to the way she was before. Lord, restore her vision so that she may have perfect sight, heal her brain so that she may be able to speak and communicate, and please give her the use of her limbs so that she may one day walk. I know she is in your hands, dear God, and I pray that you keep her safe. Thank you for all the blessings you have given us. Thank you so much. In Jesus' name I pray. Amen.

After that Steven must have told the nurses about my eye-opening experience, because they began to reduce my pain medications every two hours. They told Steven the doctors wanted to see how I would react off the drugs. They wanted to conduct neuro checks.

The same doctor who had discussed the tracheotomy and gastrostomy the day before entered the room. "The operating room is slammed so we will have to postpone the procedure until Monday. But I heard she opened her eyes. We may not even need to do the operation if she wakes up."

"That would be great," Steven said. "Thank you."

That evening the night nurse came into my room.

She told Steven that the neuro checks were to see if I would have the ability to respond to their commands. She then spoke directly to me.

"Michelle, I'd like you to move your toes and squeeze my hand. Can you do that for me?"

I knew I was being tested and I wanted to get an "A." It took all of my strength, but I moved my left toes and squeezed the nurse's hand on command. My eyes were closed and I still couldn't open them, but by the enthusiasm in her voice, I knew I had passed.

From that point, every two hours a nurse would enter the room and attempt to make me move my leg or squeeze their hands. Each time, their requests required a seemingly small task, but I knew having the correct response was an enormous victory in my recovery. During one of the checks, a night nurse informed Steven that she never got attached to patients in the ICU, since they came and went so often. But as she was sleeping during the day, she suddenly awoke and all she could think about was if I was okay. Hearing her say that touched me.

Steven then told her that he'd talked with a high school friend of mine who'd had a dream that I was in my hospital room, dressed in my normal clothes. I was smiling, talking to her as I sat at the edge of the bed, getting ready to tell everyone about my experience and how God brought me through it.

He then lovingly clasped my hand and spoke directly to me. "I know you've touched so many people throughout your life, Michelle," he said. "But this whole ordeal has made me realize that even in your deep sleep, you're still touching lives. I know you're going to pull through. I know God is going to heal you, and he's going to use this event to make a difference in the world. I just know it, Michelle."

17

THE AWAKENING

Saturday. Day eight. At around eleven in the morning, I opened my eyes and was able to keep them open. When the nurse discovered my new state, she smiled brightly.

"Let me call your husband. He's just gone to get a snack in the cafeteria. He'll be so excited to see you!"

Within moments Steven rushed into the room, eyes wide open, a huge smile covering his face.

The nurse asked if I had pain in my head. Since I couldn't speak because of all the tubes, she told me just to answer by moving my head. I nodded yes.

"She has her vision," the nurse said to Steven. "Her eyes keep following our movements. That's good."

A doctor then entered the room and started asking me questions as well. Although I was still on life support, neurologically, the doctor told Steven that I had made remarkable improvements over the last twenty-four hours.

"Because of these changes, I no longer see the need to continue with the tracheotomy," the doctor said. "Let's plan to wean her off the breathing tube, as tolerated."

Later my mom came into the room. She was fidgety and seemed nervous.

"Can you see me, Michelle?"

I looked at her through heavy, tired eyes and nodded my head. *Yes.*

"Do you know who I am?" Her voice was soft, almost fearful that I wouldn't remember who she was.

Again I nodded my head. *Yes.*

Tears rolled down her face and she laughed.

"God has answered our prayers," she said. She sat at the edge of my bed, held my good hand, and gently caressed my cheek. "My sweet girl, I love you with all of my heart."

I closed my eyes and drifted back to sleep, comforted that my mother was at my side.

The next morning, day nine, I was breathing on my own and no longer in need of life support. So at 10:00 a.m., the doctor pulled the respirator tube. My voice was barely audible, that of a low, breathy whisper.

"Her voice is probably that way from being on the ventilator for nine days," one of the nurses explained to my mom and Steven.

I was also very limited in my ability to speak. My answer to every question was a sweet, yes, even if I intended to say no.

Mom told me about all the people who'd shown up over the nine days. "Everyone came to visit you, Michelle. Chanelle and Ian came down from San Francisco. So did Devonie and the kids. Your dad even came from Arizona.

"All your high school friends were here. Jenny from high school told the story of when her house caught on fire, and how most of her clothes suffered severe smoke damage. The next day you brought a huge bag of clothes to school for her. She said she still thinks about that all the time.

"Christy, your longtime childhood friend, has been here every day. She was here the night you went into surgery. It was awful, Michelle. The nurse brought out the red surgical bag filled with your hair. It still smelled of your Biolage shampoo." Her eyes became glossy as they filled with tears. "We stood in a circle—me, your sisters, and Christy—clutching your curls of hair, wondering if it was the last piece of you we would ever touch."

She began weeping, gripping my hand. "I love you so much," she wailed. "I am so glad you are here."

Her sobs seemed to last for minutes. She took a long deep breath, collecting herself before she continued. "Your sister Ashley is passing out silver medallions to everybody. They have an angel on them. She's telling people that if anybody can pull through this, it's you. She even had everyone write letters to you in a journal so that you could read it when you woke up. In fact, everyone was so excited when I told them the good news last night, they started to dance right there in the lobby! We weren't sure you were going to make it, but you did. You made it, Michelle." She wiped tears from her eyes. "Thank God you made it."

It was difficult for me to process everything she was saying. I just knew that God had saved me and that my mom was crying happy tears.

Hospital staff began to hear of my miraculous recovery and off-duty nurses, who had never met me, came to visit so that they could see me with their own eyes. After what I had been through, to be alive was one thing. But to be alive, alert, and oriented was another. They were amazed by my progress and astounded by my strength.

As wonderful as I was doing, I knew I wasn't out of the woods yet. In fact, I had a horrible reaction to the opiate-based drugs, namely dilaudid, which caused severe anxiety and agitation. I literally did not sleep for days, my body was shaking uncontrollably, and I had a fever of 104 degrees.

Steven kept arguing with my internist that he needed to switch my medications, but the internist insisted that my reactions were common after undergoing such intensive brain surgery. I was hallucinating. I kept seeing purple people and thought they were going to eat me.

When I did sleep, I would awaken to nightmares about work or taking my comprehensive exam. One afternoon I woke up from one of my long, drug-induced naps and said, "I'm fired! I'm fired! I'm fired!" Here I was having the fight of my life and I was concerned that I'd be fired from my job. I knew I hadn't been to work in a long time, and I never called in sick. I was worried about my hospice patients. I wanted to be sure they were okay without me.

During those moments, the only thing that brought me comfort was prayer, and those who were with me witnessed the power of God's Word and work in my healing. As my father-in-law, a pastor, read Psalms 91 to 103 and Hebrews 4, I immediately relaxed and asked to hear more. As he continued, I was able to fall back asleep.

I opened my eyes and there were warm glowing candles all around the room. My mother-in-law, Patti, was speaking in tongues, my father-in-law was praying and so was Steven. I felt their hands on me, and the healing energy that flowed from their body to mine. I thought for a moment that I was back in the *Place of Prayers*; the place where soft light and worship consumed my soul, lifting my very being, providing remarkable relief and comfort. But I was confused because in that place, people didn't exist in the physical form. I opened my eyes wider and the candles disappeared, but as long as they prayed, the feeling of serenity stayed with me. When they would stop, I would again become agitated.

Although prayer brought me brief moments of peace, Steven was fed up with my constant state of unease and had a few words with the hospital staff. He challenged the doctors almost every day about the opium-based drugs, but they would not listen. He was my advocate, my protector.

On day eleven, I was feeling especially restless. I lay on the hard hospital bed wanting to get up and leave. I tried, but I couldn't move. I was helpless, like a newborn baby, totally dependent upon others to care for me. I didn't even have the strength to lift my head, and it hung there as though it were a tether ball dangling from a frayed rope. I lifted my left hand to my nose and felt plastic tubes, which irritated me. I thought it was oxygen, and assumed I could easily take it out. So I began to pull it. To my surprise and horror, I could feel the tubes coming up from my stomach, through my throat, and out of my nose, which caused me to gag a little. I thought about stopping, but I had already gone too far. I kept pulling and pulling and pulling. The slimy plastic tubes were moving through me, tickling my stomach, scratching my throat. Still, I continued to pull until I had completely removed the tube, letting it fall from my fingers to the floor next to my bed. No one was with me in the room and the effort took all of my strength.

About a half hour later two nurses came in for their routine checks and were shocked to discover I had pulled out my feeding tube. I awoke a few hours later to find the tube reinserted and taped to my upper lip with both of my hands tied to the sides of the bed.

The next morning, day twelve, a speech pathologist visited me and gave me a swallow test. The woman presented me with a small amount of what looked like sherbet ice cream and scooped up a tiny portion with a little plastic spoon. She then placed the spoon in my mouth and asked me to swallow. I did as she instructed and immediately began coughing uncontrollably, trying to catch my breath, wheezing for air. My throat felt so dry, as if there was not enough saliva to allow the food to go down smoothly.

"It's okay, Michelle," she said as she placed her hand on my back. "We'll try again later. I will allow you to have ice, though."

At least that was something. "The puree and solids will have to wait and the feeding tube will remain in place for a while," she said.

An anesthesiologist finally switched me to a different morphine-based pain medication, which allowed me to get a couple hours of sleep, but I experienced extreme sweating with a high fever as I was detoxing from the drugs. Even with the new medication, I continued having the same side effects. Opium-based medications are the only pain medications that can be injected into an IV, and because I still was unable to swallow, our options were limited. The doctors informed me that once I passed the throat test, I might be able to take pain medication orally. It gave me something important to work toward.

Through his constant vigilance about the pain medications, I could see Steven's conviction that I was going to heal completely and it meant a lot to know my husband was that passionate about my life getting back to normal. But even with that loyalty and belief, it was a tough time for us both. The less sleep and relaxation I received, the more the pressure would build in my brain. For the next several days I continued to have nightmares and hot flashes. And I would uncontrollably sing all night long. The last movie I saw before the stroke was *How to Lose a Guy in Ten Days* with Matthew McConaughey and Kate Hudson. Over and over I would sing the verse that Kate's character sang in the movie, "You're so vain, I bet you think this song is about you. Don't you? Don't you?" I don't think Steven took it personally. I just couldn't make my mind turn off the broken record playing.

In an altered state, it was difficult for me to understand my own reality. On day fifteen, a nurse wheeled me down the hallways of the hospital to another room where they parked my bed in a corner. I still didn't have the strength to move my head or most of my body. A young man, who must have been a nurse, stood over me. I could feel his eyes boring into my head.

"No, I don't think she's ready," he said.

In my head I was saying, *Yes! Yes! I'm ready.* I had no idea what he was going to do, but I knew that whatever it was, I would be one step closer to regaining my health.

Every half hour, over the course of the next several hours, the man would return and each time he'd say, "Nope. Not yet."

Please. I am ready. I am ready! I would think. I had never wanted something so badly, even though I had no clue what it was.

I stayed there for what must have been hours. At last one of the neurosurgeons came to my bedside with the nurse who had been saying I wasn't ready. They both peered over me, like I was some sort of science project, until the doctor said, "It's now or never." He reached over and quickly pulled something from my head. Immediately I felt the cold air infiltrate my brain before the nurse covered the hole with a bandage.

"Now that we pulled the drain tube, she needs to be transferred from surgery to recovery," the neurosurgeon instructed the nurse.

Victory! I thought as my heart pounded with excitement, and I loved this physician for his boldness.

The experience took a lot of energy and I soon fell asleep. I began to awaken when I sensed someone's presence. I slowly opened my eyes to find a member of the hospital staff. With his unassuming demeanor and the eyes of an angel, he watched over me while I slept. He was leaning against the wall directly in front of me, wearing blue scrubs, and holding a disposable Starbucks coffee cup. He lifted the cup to his lips and took a swig, just as he caught me watching him. He jerked slightly as if surprised, which caused coffee to dribble down the front on his chest. It made me smile.

Yes! He likes Starbucks, and as I often do, he wears it on his shirt.

But he didn't attempt to clean the mess; he didn't care, because he was focused on me. We looked at each other for a few seconds, which seemed like minutes, but didn't say a word. His aura was a glowing yellow, the same beautiful colors I had seen in the *Place of Prayers*, and I knew instantly that this was the man who saved my life. I had never seen an aura before, but now it was as though I had the ability to see people's hearts—to know their true intentions and understand their purpose. God had used this man's hands to perform a miracle, removing the lesion in my brain that I had always been told was inoperable.

Finally, he walked closer to the bed. "I'm Dr. William Dobkin. I was the neurosurgeon who worked on you when you first came in." He took a deep breath, "You know," he said, followed by a long thoughtful pause. "It was touch and go there for a while. But you are doing remarkably well."

I smiled. I knew he must be trying to make sense of why I wasn't in worse shape. I knew that most people who suffered from massive strokes had extremely poor outcomes, in which they were unable to see or comprehend language. I wanted to tell him how I was wrapped in God's infinite love, lifted by his gentle arms to receive complete healing through the countless prayers that poured over my soul, and that he was the angel on earth who was called to save my life on that rainy, fateful, Friday night. I wanted to thank him, to let him know that his work was good, and that all the long hours he put in were worth more than he could ever imagine. But my damaged brain couldn't find the words. So I just smiled, he humbly smiled back, nodded, and walked out of the room.

Soon thereafter the speech therapist entered the room and conducted another swallow test. It felt as though I was back in school and the pressure was on. I needed to hear that I was doing a great job! That's me. I have always thrived on praise and positive feedback.

"All right, Michelle, I am going to give you some applesauce to see if you can swallow. Are you ready?"

In a soft whisper, I responded, "Yes."

Slowly into my mouth went the applesauce, which sat on a tiny plastic spoon. I swallowed, which triggered another dramatic coughing fit, causing the food that was once in my mouth to be spit up all over my hospital gown. When I had calmed down, and could breathe normally again, the therapist patiently said, "Are we ready to try again?"

"Yes," I whispered.

"This time, try not to cough."

Another mouthful of applesauce. Slowly and carefully I swallowed, feeling the cool, sweet slush slide down my throat. Another victory and I rejoiced, savoring each mouthful, until I had finished the entire serving.

"Great job, Michelle! We are ready to remove the feeding tube. You can now eat on your own!" I was thrilled, but didn't have the energy to express my excitement. So instead, I fell back into a peaceful sleep knowing that everything was going to be okay.

When I awoke, I was back in my room in ICU. Steven came to my bedside and held my hand.

"How are you feeling?"

I half smiled.

"They removed the drain tube and the feeding tube," Steven said with excitement. "The doctor said that after suffering such a catastrophic stroke, you are making a remarkable recovery. They'll continue to monitor your progress for the likelihood of a cerebral shunt, which he said is a surgical procedure used to treat hydrocephalus, or a buildup of fluid on the brain. But he said with the rate that you're going, you may not even need one. That's good news! You are making huge improvements."

Because I could now swallow, my pain medications were changed from intravenous to oral, and aside from being awakened by a few hot flashes, I was finally able to get some sleep. But before I drifted off, I began to ask Steven questions that I knew the answers to but had to hear again.

"What happened?" I whispered.

Steven had to lean in close, placing his ear inches from my face to understand what I was saying.

"You had a stroke. Do you remember going to the fire station?"

"Yes."

"Do you remember being in the emergency room?"

I tried to think. I tried to remember, but the only thing I could recall was the place of all the prayers. A place filled with a soft, warm, glowing light of which I was a part, with songs of praise sung in every language, creating a healing hum that reverberated through my soul.

"Do you know what kind of surgery they did?"

I looked at him again.

"Dr. Dobkin removed the AVM. It's completely gone, Michelle," he said as his voice cracked with emotion.

I started to cry, but my eyes wouldn't produce tears, so my face crinkled up. I imagined that I probably looked like a Shar-Pei, as my lip began to quiver. I lifted my hand to touch my head and felt that it was covered in bandages, creating a small turban-like cap.

"Don't touch your head, Michelle!" Steven exclaimed as he grabbed my good hand and held it in his. "Why are you crying? There is nothing to worry about anymore. Everything is going to be okay."

"Is work okay with me taking time off for the surgery?"

Steven laughed. "Yes, don't worry about it."

"How long have I been in the hospital?"

"A little more than two weeks."

"What about school?"

"I had your friends turn in your thesis so you passed the class. When you recover more, you can take the research class you still need to graduate and Tammara and Mary said they would help you study for the comprehensive exam."

I began to cry again, or attempted to anyways.

"Michelle, please don't cry. Everything will be fine, I promise." He looked at me with genuine affection, his rough, large hands still holding mine, and slowly lifted my hand to his lips, giving it a tender, loving kiss. "When you get out of the hospital, you can have whatever you want."

"You better watch what you say!" I whispered through a sniffle.

Steven laughed again and I smiled.

I looked at my sweet, strong husband. Although he wore a huge smile, I noticed that he looked thinner and had dark circles under his eyes.

"Have you been here the whole time?" I whispered.

He nodded. "I've slept here every night and been here every day. I only leave you once a day to go home and shower."

No wonder you look exhausted, I thought.

I lay in a hospital bed for sixteen days, half of which time a ventilator kept me alive. Some may have written me off, but Steven, and most important, God, never did. And in spite of all I had been through, my memory was strong, I could speak, I could see, and one day, I knew I would walk again.

18

A DOSE OF FRIENDSHIP

On day seventeen, I opened my eyes to find myself in an unfamiliar room. Steven came to my side, leaned in close, and soothingly held my hand.

"They moved you from ICU. You are getting better, so you're in a regular room."

I looked around and saw an enormous window that overlooked Newport's harbor. The sun glistened off the water on one of the clearest days I had ever seen. I breathed out a sigh of relief; it overjoyed me to see the outside world again. I was relaxed, I was healing, and I knew that soon, I would be going home.

"You have an angiogram scheduled today to determine if they got everything during the surgery," he continued.

I knew what an angiogram was. I had undergone that procedure a dozen times before since I was diagnosed at the age of eleven. I knew that I would be semi-sedated, that a soft catheter would be inserted into the main artery of my groin and guided through my body to my neck where an iodine dye would be injected, making the veins in the brain show clearly on the x-ray pictures.

"Everyone has really been pulling for you. The next door neighbors have been watching our dog, Bear. People I don't even know have been sending get well cards and flowers. Prayer chains have been started and your friends have offered to donate their hair for a wig. So many people love you, Michelle."

I started to cry, but again, my eyes weren't capable of producing tears.

"Do you want visitors?"

I nodded.

"Your mom and your sisters have gone back to the mountain, so do you want me to call Christy?"

I smiled and nodded again.

"Okay. The doctors said that you can only have visitors for a half hour at a time so that you don't get too worn out."

Steven then called my friend Christy and asked her if she wanted to stop over. I could hear her yell yes through the phone and that she would come immediately.

About an hour after he invited her to come, the door slowly opened. I looked over, our eyes met, and I knew who she was. Christy's eyes filled with tears and she ran to the bed and hugged me tightly.

"I wasn't sure you'd remember me."

"Christy!" I said in my strained whisper-like voice, before breaking into silent sobs, crying quietly because my voice was gone, yet still unable to produce tears. She crawled onto the bed and cuddled next to me.

"Michelle," Steven said, laughing, "Why are you crying?"

Christy and I both ignored him and continued interacting only like friends of twenty years could. She opened a bag filled with old photos of me growing up, of us together, with her sister Sarah.

"Mom and I gathered these. We weren't sure how much you'd remember or if you'd remember at all." I loved seeing all the pictures and remembered all of the events and people they had captured.

"We weren't sure you were going to make it," Christy said quietly. "During the early part of your time here, your mom asked me to write your eulogy, which I did. That was rough." She smiled as the tears streamed down her face.

Steven then arranged for my friends, Tammara and Mary from grad school, to come see me. For the first fifteen minutes of the visit, we cried and then laughed at the fact that we couldn't stop crying. At least I was making the gestures as if I were crying, with intense emotion behind my facial grimacing. Like Christy, they expressed the same relief that I was alive and my memory was strong.

Tammara was a beauty queen: Miss Anaheim, Miss Seal Beach, and a cheerleader for the Anaheim Ducks ice hockey team. She always looked fabulous. When I first met her, although I was struck by her beauty, I was more instantly drawn to her sense of humor and her kind heart. She was always giving me styling tips, which I appreciated, and God knows I needed.

"Does my shaved head look bad?" I knew I could count on her honest opinion.

"If Britney Spears could pull it off, then anyone could."

We both laughed.

"I brought you a basket full of treats and magazines so you can catch up on all the things that have happened while you were in your coma."

We flipped through *People* magazine while she brought me up to date on all the Hollywood gossip. Tom Cruise and Katie Holmes's new relationship was all the rage, and we looked at the latest fashion trends, collecting ideas for short hair styles.

"What about school?" I asked.

Mary replied, "I turned in your thesis and we just took the comprehensive exam. But don't worry, you passed the class and we will totally help you study for the test." Mary was in her early fifties and was the regional director of human resources for Kaiser Permanente.

"I will give you all my study notes for the test. You will pass, Michelle. I know it!" Tammara chimed in. They were referring to the six-hour exam that all students were required to pass along with the completion of a thesis.

Sitting at my bedside, Tammara turned serious. "I came to the hospital the day after you had your stroke. It was the most horrible feeling I've ever had. There was so much sadness, so much doubt, and so much hopelessness. For the first time I thought that this may be your time to go. I told my mom, 'I don't want to think of living in a world that Michelle isn't in.'

"My mom told me, 'Then fight for Michelle like she would fight for you, pray for her life like she would pray for yours, and believe that she will survive like she would believe for you.' From that moment on, I never again felt afraid that you weren't going to come back to this world. I just waited patiently for the day that you would. Today is that day."

19

LEARNING TO LIVE

The following day, a nurse entered the room. She took my blood pressure, checked my IVs, gave me more pain medication, and then began the neuro checks.

"What year is it, Michelle?"

I thought about it. "1982."

"No, that's the year you were born."

"1994?"

"No. Try again."

Disappointment overwhelmed me. *I used to be so smart*, I thought. I again began to cry, crinkling my nose, contorting my face, making silent sobs, but still unable to produce tears.

"It's okay, Michelle," the nurse said gently. "I don't even know what year it is half the time. Do you know what day it is?"

I looked around my room and saw a white board where someone had written, "Today is January 22."

"January 22," I replied.

"That's okay, you can look. Very good, Michelle!"

The fact that I could still read and find meaning in words was a tremendous sign of improvement.

Steven asked me if I wanted to take a picture of us together. I nodded.

"I'll take it," the nurse offered.

She snapped the photo and handed the camera back to Steven. He hit the preview button and I saw what I looked like for the first time in three weeks. I was twenty pounds lighter, my head was shaved, my eyes sunken to the back of my sockets, and the left side of my head was indented from where my skull cap was removed and then replaced with a metal plate. But I looked surprisingly alert. The stroke affected my right arm and leg, but I still had perfect symmetry in my face. My smile radiated beauty back at me and I now had the strength to hold up my head.

Looking at the photo made me more emotional, causing more silent, mournful sobs as I realized I had just had the fight of my life.

Soon the speech therapist entered the room and conducted another swallow test, this time with solid foods. After several successful bites of fruit, she asked if I would like a meal from the cafeteria.

"Yes, that would be lovely," I replied.

Since I had come out of my coma, I was using words that I would typically never say during conversation. I even asked one of the pregnant nurses if she was "with child." Who talks like that? I know I never did before the stroke. But now I was more sophisticated, extremely polite, and I always thanked the nurses and doctors when they came to check on me. After all, I was completely dependent upon them to care for me and I owed them my life.

One of the hospital staff brought a tray to my room and placed it on the bedside table. Steven lifted the cover and I smelled a delicious food—meatloaf. My mouth watered. I hadn't had a hot meal in weeks and I was ready to dig in, but I just looked at it.

"Eat, Michelle. You can do it," he said.

I was thinking about how one eats. *How do I get the food in my mouth?* I knew there were steps to take, but I didn't know what they were. I thought and thought, but I couldn't remember. I had no idea what to do, so I looked to Steven for help.

"Put the food in your mouth," he instructed.

I had to think about where my mouth was located on my body, where the food was located in front of me, and how to get the food from the plate into my mouth. After several seconds, I used my fingers on my left hand and scooped up a handful of meatloaf and shoved it in my mouth.

"Use the fork, Michelle! Like this." Steven demonstrated and took a bite of the meatloaf, which made him cringe. It wasn't bad; he just hates meatloaf, which made me smile.

Steven put the fork in my hand and I attempted to stab at the meatloaf. When I was finally able to get a piece, I tried to bring the fork to my mouth, but missed. After several failed attempts, I gave up and began shoveling the food in my mouth with my hand as fast as I could. Steven ran to get the nurse who had moved on to another patient, but by the time he returned, my plate had been licked dry and there was meatloaf smeared across my face.

Steven and the nurse gave each other a look.

"I'll call the occupational therapist," the nurse said. "She will help her relearn the activities of daily living."

The next afternoon I awoke from a nap to discover my uncle John sitting in a chair at my bedside reading. He lowered his newspaper, just enough so I could see his eyes peering over at me.

"Well, hey, sweet. How ya doing?" He set the paper down and came over to the edge of my bed and sat.

"Uncle John?" I whispered, not believing it was really him.

"Yes, dear, it's me," he said as tears welled up in his eyes. He took both of my hands in his and squeezed tightly before moving in and giving me a long kiss on the forehead. He pulled away and smiled.

"You have had quite a time, haven't you?"

"Yes," I exhaled. "Was I sleeping long?"

"No, only about a half hour or so."

"I'm sorry."

"Don't be sorry. I would have let you sleep all day. But I wasn't going to leave until we had the chance to see each other."

He gazed at me and I saw pure love in his eyes. Finally he stood and walked to the window. "Wow, this is really a lovely room. You have quite a view."

I smiled.

Walking back toward the bed he asked, "How are you feeling? You look good."

"Fine," I responded. It was difficult for me to give more than one word answers and when I did speak in sentences, they were extremely simple.

"What's on your legs, Michelle?"

I looked toward the foot of my bed where I saw giant boots on both of my legs, which I had never noticed before.

"I don't know!" I became very agitated and wanted them off.

"Hold on, sweet. Let me go get a nurse."

I continued to squirm, but I was still weak and did not have the strength to sit up and lean forward, let alone remove two large plastic boots from my feet.

A nurse entered the room with Uncle John trailing behind her.

"Do you want your boots off, Michelle?"

"Yes," I softly replied.

"What purpose do the boots serve?" Uncle John asked. "They look like black moon shoes."

The nurse undid the Velcro and began removing the boots. "They keep her feet stretched so that her toes don't point downward. This will help her to walk again. In fact, the physical therapist should be stopping by sometime today. We are going to try to get you out of bed."

Once the boots were removed, my hairy legs were exposed, along with half painted toenails.

"It looks like you're in need of a pedicure," my uncle said. "Would you like me to arrange one for you, dear?"

"Yes," I replied.

"I know of a lovely woman who will come right here to the hospital. I'll give her a ring today and see if she can come tomorrow," he said as he sat back down in the chair.

Steven entered the room. My uncle stood to shake his hand.

"Well, hey, guy. How are things?" my uncle asked.

"Good, good. Just stressful. Work is out of control. Thanks for watching her. Her mom and Craig needed some relief so they're in the mountains and my parents couldn't make it out today. I really appreciate it."

"No problem, are you kidding me? She's a doll. So things at work aren't going so well?"

"No, no." Steven always answered questions by stating the first word of his answer twice before elaborating. "Starbucks just grew too quickly, saturating the market, and now they are closing stores. This has been a stressful three weeks. Michelle had her stroke and I have been working every day from the hospital and sleeping here at night. I have already been through two rounds of layoffs. If I lose my job, we'll lose our health insurance. I just don't know how much more I can take."

"Well, I'll give it to you, guy, you've done one hellava job."

"The economy is tanking, and I just don't know. I have several renovations going on right now and I have to tour stores." As the Starbucks Facilities and Renovations Manager for Orange County, it was important for Steven to be out in the field.

"I hear ya. Everyone's portfolio is down. Everyone is running scared." Uncle John looked back at me and smiled. "You know," he said. "I noticed that Michelle could use a pedicure. Would it be okay if I send someone over to give her one?"

Steven looked over to me, but I was already half asleep.

"Yeah, yeah. I think she would like that."

"Very good, then. Listen, I will let you be. Michelle needs her rest and it sounds like you could use some too. I'll be back tomorrow, hopefully with my friend to give the pedicure."

"Okay, that sounds great. Thank you, Uncle John."

"You are very welcome. Ciao," he said as he waved goodbye and walked out the door.

An hour or so passed when two new people entered the room.

"Michelle, wake up," the woman said abruptly. "It's time to get out of bed."

I groggily opened my eyes to see an older Caucasian lady with brown short hair and a younger, slightly overweight Filipino man with a walker at his side.

"What are you doing?" Steven asked.

"I'm a physical therapist, this is my aide, and we need to get Michelle walking again."

The aide was holding a walker as if they were ready for me to walk out of the joint.

Since waking from my coma, I was very in tune with people's energy. I knew when they were in a sour mood, if their intentions were good, if they were bad, if I should be careful. Maybe it was a sixth sense or an animal instinct, but it was as though I had the ability to discern people's motivations. It was a sense of knowing that I had acquired in the *Place of Prayers* and was the method that God now used to speak to me.

This therapist was exhausted; burnt out. She wanted to retire but couldn't afford to. She didn't tell me this, but somehow I knew. The gentleman at her side was just there to do his job and was happy to be receiving a paycheck.

Her negative energy made me instantly uncooperative.

"Come on, Michelle," the woman said.

And without a choice, she propped me up and swung my legs over the side of the bed. I immediately became dizzy and started shaking, as I felt the blood rushing from my head down to my toes. The gentleman quickly put the walker in front of me, while she put a large cloth belt around my waist.

"Grab the handles on the walker. I'll hold you up!" And she lifted me by the belt from the back to a standing position. Unprepared, I was terrified and began to cry. I just looked at the walker and didn't move, so the gentleman grabbed my left hand and placed it on the walker and secured my stroke hand to the handle with some kind of brace.

I began to hyperventilate. "It's okay, Michelle. Just take a few steps. One foot in front of the other," the therapist instructed.

My entire body was tingling as if I had slept in an uncomfortable position that had caused me to lose circulation. It felt like I was being stabbed with a million little knives all over my body and the pain only heightened my fear.

"Don't worry, we got you. You are not going to fall."

At this point, real, wet, salty tears were streaming down my face. I became excited that I could actually cry, but wanted desperately to get back in bed. I wasn't ready to walk. I looked to Steven for help.

"It's okay, Michelle," Steven said. He has always pushed me to go further, encouraging me to be the best I could be, even when I wanted to give up.

The woman bent down and began moving my feet. Sliding the left foot forward, followed by the right. "Very good, Michelle! You just took two steps. Do you want to try more or do you want to go back to bed?"

"Bed," I whimpered.

"Look at you," Steven said, smiling. "You're a fighter, Michelle. Great job!"

I was still upset for having to do something I didn't want to.

"We'll come back tomorrow and do this again," the therapist said as she helped me back into bed.

"No!" I hoarsely whispered. "I don't want to. I'm not ready."

"Are you sure?" the woman asked. "It will help you get better faster."

"No. I don't want to," I cried. "Don't make me do it." The truth of it was that I didn't like her and I didn't want to be in her presence.

"Okay, Michelle," Steven said. "Don't worry. We'll just take it day by day."

I was relieved.

The following morning Uncle John entered my room with his friend who had her tackle box in hand. He introduced her, but I quickly forgot her name.

She pulled up a chair and sat at the edge of my bed, placing the tackle box in her lap. Uncle John stood behind her, squeezed both of her shoulders, and said, "This gal is a doll and she will fix up your toes so that they're all nice and pretty."

"What color would you like?" the woman asked.

"Pink."

"Would you like me to bring the box so that you can look at the options?"

"No. Pink please."

She took the polish off the toes on my left foot, which tickled a bit. The pungent smell of the nail polish remover infiltrated my nostrils and gave me a slight headache. She then moved to my right foot. The minute she touched my toes, my right leg went stiff, as if it were over-reacting to the stimulus, yet I could barely feel her touching me.

"Are you okay?" she asked.

"My feeling seems different on that leg," I said concerned.

"Remember they said you lost about 60 percent of your sensation on your right side?" Steven said.

I looked at him trying to remember.

"They have been running so many tests. Don't worry about it. You will be fine."

"We're almost done," the woman chimed in. "Soon you will have the most beautiful toes in all of Hoag Hospital! Just one more toe and we will be good to go."

I drifted back off to sleep.

When I awoke, Uncle John and his friend were gone. The doctors began discussing the discharge options with Steven and me. I could go to a rehab hospital for a few weeks or go home and receive Home Health services.

I wanted to go home.

20

GOING HOME

On Friday, January 25, 2008, after twenty-one days in the hospital—sixteen days in ICU and five days in the stroke ward—I was discharged to go home. The durable medical equipment was delivered to my house where our neighbors set everything up: a hospital bed, bedside commode, shower chair, a walker, and a wheelchair.

Before I left the hospital, the nurses removed my catheter and gave me a gallon of water to drink in an attempt to make me urinate. But no matter how hard I tried, nothing would come out. A series of different nurses tested various tactics to get the flow going. One took a crack at running the water faucet in the room as she tapped her foot anxiously on the floor. Another tried playing soothing music. Still another endeavored to give me more fluid. Nothing worked. So they stuck the catheter back in and called an ambulance for transport.

Steven and I were both surprised. Although we had discussed discharge options, we didn't think that it would be the next day. I wasn't ready to go home and Steven wasn't prepared to care for me.

"I can't believe it," Steven said.

"They dropped me like a hot potato," I whispered.

Steven laughed. "Well, you haven't lost your sense of humor, that's for sure."

When the paramedics arrived, they loaded me onto a gurney, and asked if I wanted to be wrapped up like a taco or a burrito.

"Wrap me up like a burrito please," I replied.

They wrapped me in a blanket, strapped my body to the gurney, and down the hall we went until I felt the cool fresh air of the winter night hit my face. Once in the ambulance, all the bumps in the road hurt my head and I wanted the ride to be over.

I was tired and could barely open my eyes, but I definitely kept them open when we got to my house. The outside of the house was decorated with light-up balloons and a banner spanned the width of the garage that read, "Welcome Home, Michelle."

"The neighbors did this," Steven told me. "They wanted you to know how much they support you." I was overwhelmed by their kindness. After all, we had only lived in the neighborhood for less than six months.

For the first several nights, I slept in a hospital bed in my living room. Looking out the family room window onto a street filled with life, longing to feel the sun on my skin, I finally understood what my hospice patients felt like. Free of pain, but totally dependent on others to care for them. Helpless. Bed-bound. Confined to a single room. Weak. Wounded. Vulnerable. Anxious. And I finally understood the power of touch, and what it meant to have someone hold your hand. To be present and in the moment, without having to fill the space with meaningless chatter. I realized that when someone is critically ill, there is something so significant about just being present. I didn't have the energy to speak. I didn't know how to count past ten. Or how to spell. I couldn't comprehend more than one or two sentences at a time. All I wanted was a calming presence to be there. And in that moment, in that hospital bed, in my living room, I knew why God saved me. With every inch of my being, I knew that I had to continue dedicating the rest of my life to serving those who are dying. I had to return to my hospice work so that I could live out my purpose.

On Sunday morning, Steven put my laptop in front of me and told me to start typing. I had no idea what a laptop was and I began touching the icons on the screen, intuitively thinking that my gestures would make something happen. In my brain, it didn't make sense to punch the buttons on the keyboard to control the content on the screen.

Our neighbors began a dinner rotation where each night at 6:00 p.m., a different family would bring us a home-cooked meal. I know it was a huge relief to Steven and it helped me learn how to eat with a fork and spoon again.

Some of Steven's construction buddies built a temporary wheel-chair ramp outside our back door. About a week before I had my stroke, one of my hospice patients passed away and the family donated an electric scooter to our organization. I couldn't find a patient who would benefit, so I brought it home to sell online knowing the money could help a patient in another way. What a blessing that scooter turned out to be. Once the wheelchair ramp was installed, the electric scooter gave me an incredible amount of independence. I could move about the house and go for walks with our dog without having to rely on someone to push me in a wheelchair.

The wounds on my head hadn't quite scabbed and they constantly oozed. My skin was also terribly dry over those first few weeks after coming home. My friend Christy, who stayed with me several times a week while Steven was working, would spend at least fifteen minutes each visit giving me a lotion massage. My skin peeled off my entire body like it had been badly sunburned. I have no idea why. Christy would help peel it off a little at a time and we did moisturizing face masks together while I lay in the hospital bed. For her, the hardest part of her time with me was when I would ask her what happened. I would then ask if I almost died. My short term memory was very poor, so I asked the same difficult questions each time we were together and each time she'd give the same, patient answers.

"You had a massive stroke and the doctors had no choice but to do emergency brain surgery. You were in a coma for eight days and we didn't think you were going to make it. Not Steven, though. He was determined that you would pull through. I remember praying, 'Lord, please bring her back to us the way she was before, or else please take her home.' Our prayers were answered, Michelle. You are here and you are still you!"

Each time she told the story, I would cry silent sobs, like the ones she saw when she came to visit me in the stroke ward, but now there were actually tears.

We watched TV, talked, ate McDonalds, and drank Starbucks together. We would cry, reminisce, and with the scooter, we would take Bear for walks. We read CaringBridge together and I reconnected with some old friends from our childhood. But mostly, we just enjoyed each other's company.

At first, I could only stay awake for about twenty minutes at a time. I would always apologize for needing to take a nap, but Christy would remind me that sleep was what I needed to heal.

The most encouraging times we had together began when the physical therapist started coming to the house. Steven came home from work for my first session. He helped me strap a neoprene brace on my right foot that he bought at the drugstore. This would have to suffice until the orthopedist had a custom one made. I absolutely loved my physical therapist, Sabrina. She was young like me; petite, fair skinned with freckles, and was always smiling. She came in and met our dog, who rambunctiously greeted every houseguest. Holding him back by the collar, Steven introduced him. "I apologize. This is our dog, Bear. Let me go throw him out back."

Sabrina petted him and said, "Hi, Bear!"

I repeated her word for word. "Hi, Bear!" What I meant to say was hello to her, but that's not what came out. I felt so stupid. I used to be so smart and now I was just repeating everything, like a toddler. But Sabrina's smile was glowing and when she walked through the door, she came right to me, sat on my bedside, and said, "Hi, Michelle. I'm Sabrina, your physical therapist. I'm here to help you recover, and today, you are going to walk!"

I looked at her like she was crazy.

How is this tiny little woman ever going to have the strength to help me stand? After my first experience in the hospital, the idea of walking made me so nervous, I began to visibly shake.

"I am going to put this belt around you." She sat by my side and placed my good arm around her neck.

"Are you ready? One, two, three, up you go!"

Before I had the chance to object, I was already standing on my own two feet, clinging to Sabrina's side for stability.

"Very good, Michelle. Great job! Now you're going to take a few steps forward. I gotcha."

I took my first step.

"Very good!"

"Look at that! Look at that. Great job, hon!" Steven exclaimed. "Let me grab the catheter bag," he said as he unhooked the bag from the side of the bed.

"Now take all your weight off your left foot and place it on your right," Sabrina instructed. The floor seemed a long way away from where I was standing, but I had to keep going. I had to.

I moved slowly, shuffling my way forward, inch by inch.

"Look at that!" Steven kept shouting. He was so excited. I was scared, but in spite of that fear, I was able to complete a circle around my living room with Sabrina holding me up as if we were slow dancing, Steven following me with the catheter bag, Christy videotaping, standing behind the camera. It was a small lap of victory and my team was incredibly supportive, cheering me on the entire way.

"Can you feel where we are in space?" Sabrina asked as we were coming back to the bed.

"Yeah," I whispered.

"Okay, good."

"Backing up is harder, but we'll do it. Lean this way," Sabrina directed as she slowly guided me to the edge of the bed. "Very good!"

"Very good!" I repeated.

"Look at that! You walked in that whole circle," Steven said, grinning ear to ear.

Once I got moving, there was no stopping me. Sabrina had a walker adapted with a special handle that I could grip with my right hand. Now that I was walking, my whole demeanor changed and I was truly cheerful again. I was smiling, laughing, and cracking jokes. During one visit, Sabrina commented on how beautiful I looked in my wedding picture hanging on the wall.

"Yes, I was quite a southern belle. One hot mama!"

Everyone laughed as I continued practicing walking with her, making it out the front door and up and down the sidewalk in front of our house. Being able to walk again gave me such a confidence boost. I knew I was on my way and it was a glorious feeling.

A couple days later, my occupational therapist began her visits, which occurred three times a week. She taught me how to brush my teeth, shower, shave my legs and armpits, put on a bra, and dress myself. I learned how to do these same tasks with one hand when I was twelve years old, so I knew I could learn how to do them again. The only difference was that I was much more disabled than I'd ever been before. Since I was twelve years old, I had always walked with a limp and was unable to use my right hand. Now, I could barely walk at all and was suffering from severe spasticity. The muscles on my right side had hyperactive reflexes and uncontrollable shaking that was difficult to cope with. Before, my spasticity had been relatively mild and was only triggered by quick movements or exhaustion. Now, my muscles were in a constant state of spasticity, which, I learned, is often found in people who suffer a catastrophic stroke or sustain a traumatic brain injury. As a result, the doctor prescribed Botox injections in both my right arm and my leg to help relax the muscles. Believe it or not, Botox was originally invented to treat such conditions, until the plastic surgeons got a hold of it and started using it to treat wrinkles.

I also had a visiting nurse whose goals were to get me urinating independently and keep my bowel movements regular, both of which proved to be extremely difficult tasks. My poor friends and family! All I ever talked about was going to the bathroom, not because I had to go, but because I wanted to go. It became "normal" for me to go "number two" once every five days and the constipation caused great discomfort. The nurse put me on a regular regime of prune juice and stool softeners, but it didn't help that one of the main side effects from all my medications was constipation.

The nurse also referred me to a urologist who gave us the tools needed to wean me off a catheter, an agonizingly slow process. Whenever I had to pee, I would have to call Steven, who would come home from work, manually insert the catheter and let the fluid flow into the bed pan. It was incredibly awkward, but as uncomfortable as it was, Steven was the only person I would let help me with this problem. At this point, he was going through the fifth round of layoffs and it wasn't the most opportune time for him to be running home from work so that his wife could go to the bathroom. I sensed his frustration and it made me work even harder to get my life back. I would try to drink as little as possible throughout the day, and when I knew I had to go, I would sit on the toilet for what felt like hours with the faucet running. Each time nothing would happen and each time the disappointment seemed to consume me.

Calling Steven was difficult in more ways than one. Not only did he sound frustrated with me each time he had to leave work, but I also didn't understand what numbers meant or how phone numbers worked when they were dialed in a particular sequence. To solve this problem, Steven had to put his number on speed dial in my cell phone, so that whenever I held down the number *1*, it would call his number. I remember practicing how to dial a phone number by calling my mom's home phone, the number I had known since I was a child, which I could recite verbally, but was unable to press on the keypad. I tried over and over and over, at least thirty times, until my mom finally answered the phone. In a quiet whisper I exclaimed, "Mom!" She started screaming shouts of excitement when she realized it was me and that I had dialed the number on my own.

Christy took me to one of my first follow-up appointments with my neurosurgeon, Dr. Dobkin. We arrived a half hour early, which was a good thing because it took fifteen minutes to get a handicap parking spot and another fifteen minutes for Christy to figure out how to open the collapsible wheelchair and get me in it. We made our way to his office and were quickly taken back to see him. To Christy, Dr. Dobkin looked so different from how she remembered him on the night of my surgery. He looked rested and encouraged to see me, not exhausted and without hope. To me, his aura continued to shine. I gave him a thank you card with a fifty dollar Starbucks gift card in it. It was the least I could do to show him my appreciation for saving my life. He shook his head in disbelief at my progress.

"Anyone who reads your case file would not expect to see you coming through that door. You, Michelle, talking, perfect vision, moving, remembering. Amazing," he said. "People just don't come out of what you went through."

I looked at him, smiled, and whispered, "It's a miracle."

He thoughtfully paused, smiled, and then nodded in agreement. "Yes, it is."

After just a month, my physical therapist, Sabrina, announced that I had met all of my quarterly goals. She couldn't believe it, but I was already well enough to begin outpatient rehabilitation back at Hoag Hospital.

21

CROSSING THE THRESHOLD

On the car ride from my house back to Hoag Hospital, I looked out the passenger window and saw the blossoming plum trees, budding precious white flowers along the center divider of Newport Boulevard. As the wind blew I watched the tiny delicate blossoms fall to the ground, covering the asphalt like a thin layer of snow, and it reminded me of what heaven is like. There is evidence of God everywhere in nature.

Steven and I arrived at the outpatient rehab center where I was given a full assessment. After a series of tests, the lead therapist determined that I needed physical, occupational, and speech therapy three times a week, which were scheduled back to back so that I was in rehab for three hours at a time without a break. At the conclusion of the first visit the swelling around the incision on my skull had become so severe, I could press my finger into my head and it felt like a squeegee.

After completing my second visit, all the activity of rehab proved too much to bear. My head throbbed and my skull was leaking fluid. My stepdad, Craig, had taken me to the appointment, so he wheeled me down the hall to the emergency room where I was admitted for hydrocephalus, or water on the brain, and prescribed a series of medications, including a steroid to reduce the swelling. No one was still certain about whether or not I needed a shunt, a permanent device that would drain excess fluid and relieve pressure on my brain. I considered this only a minor setback and was released from the hospital four days later.

When I returned to rehab the next week, my faith was stronger, but my body seemed weaker. My voice was that of a soft whisper; I could barely dial a phone number, and couldn't find the words to speak more than a few short sentences. But I knew that I would be okay. I knew that everything was in God's hands. He had taken me this far, and I knew he would continue to carry me.

The point came where Steven needed a break from caregiving and I wanted to spend more time with my family. Uncle John made arrangements for everyone to stay at his place on Balboa Island. He said that everyone was welcome, so my dad drove out from Arizona, my half-sister came from the Bay area, and all of my sisters were there as well as a few close friends. Before leaving my house, Steven showed my mom how to catheterize me, but she complained that she couldn't see. All of my life she wore contacts, then she had Lasik surgery, and now she just wore glasses. The thought of her inserting the catheter in the wrong hole terrified me, but I went on the trip anyway. After our family dinner, Craig carried me up the stairs to the guest bedroom where my mom helped me get dressed for bed.

"Do you need to go to the bathroom?" my mother asked.

"Yes, but I want to try going pee by myself."

"Okay. I will help you to the toilet."

Once I was situated, I asked her to leave the room. "I need to concentrate, but can you please turn on the water before you go?"

She turned on the sink faucet and stepped just outside the door, refusing to close it in case something happened. For twenty long minutes I sat there and nothing came out.

"Do you want me to catheterize you, Michelle?"

"No, Mom. Leave me alone. I can do this."

"Are you sure?"

"Mom!"

She stepped outside and began pacing the hall. A few more minutes passed and I finally peed!

"Mom! Mom! I peed. I peed!" You would have thought I won the Olympic gold medal. My mom started screaming with excitement and yelled down the stairs, "She did it! She peed." Applause, hoots, and hollers erupted, and my sisters ran upstairs to congratulate me. Our blended family has no boundaries. It never has. My triumph was their triumph, and we were all so happy, we actually cried. And that was the end of the catheter forever as my family tucked me into bed.

In outpatient therapy, we talked a lot about goals. My speech therapist straight away asked, "What are your goals?"

"To finish school."

"Okay, what will that involve? What do you still need to do to graduate?" she asked.

"Take a research class and pass the comps."

"What are the comps?"

"The comprehensive exam, a six-hour test where you are tested on everything you've learned."

"When is the test?"

"I missed it. I was supposed to take it in January, but I was in the hospital."

"Can you take the test at a later time?"

"I don't know," I said. But it got my wheels turning that maybe this was a possibility.

"What other goals do you have?"

"To return to my hospice patients at work."

"What were some of your daily tasks at work?"

"Typing, talking, public speaking, event planning, fundraising, meeting with patients and families."

"Wow, that's quite a list. Let's see if we can't help retrain your brain on how to perform some of those higher level activities."

And so I began my speech therapy not only with vocal exercises, but also with memory tests, computer games, as well as daily, weekly, and monthly planning so that I could begin obtaining my goals. I kept a giant calendar in my kitchen so I could track my actions and work to meet deadlines that I had set for myself. In the beginning, my goals were simple, such as to brush my teeth without having to be reminded, type an email, and read a paragraph. As my brain began making more connections, I set more complex goals like walking without a walker. To meet my goals, I had to practice and prepare. I had to get myself in a routine, completing all the simple tasks each day while working toward the more difficult goals. As the days passed, seeing the tasks written on the calendar in my own handwriting, writing that looked like it was done by a seven year old, gave me a sense of accomplishment because I could look back and visibly see my progress. I could even see how my handwriting had improved over the weeks.

We thought for the longest time that my lost voice was caused by the ventilator scraping the sides of my throat. But after months with no improvement, I was referred to an ear, nose, and throat doctor who discovered that the stroke had paralyzed my vocal chord on the right side. As a result, the words I could say only came out as a hoarse whisper. The cure: talk and sing as much as possible to exercise those muscles in hopes that they would regain their strength, which I gladly did.

One day in April, my friend Tammara called and said that she was chosen to give a speech at graduation because of a story she had written about me. I told her what my speech therapist had said and that I wished I could be graduating with her. Her reply reminded me of Deanne's, my friend who encouraged me to try out for the volleyball team, when she said, "You can!" She went on to explain how, "To participate in the graduation ceremony, a student must have less than one class remaining, which you can take over the summer, and be signed up to take the comprehensive exams, which you can take in June."

"Really?"

"Yes, really! I'll help you. This is so exciting! All you have to do is go online and fill out the registration form. You can also order your cap and gown online."

With Tammara's help, I was able to register for the comprehensive exam along with my research class, and sign up to participate in the graduation ceremony in May. She tutored me nearly every day in order to help me prepare for the exam and gave me all of her note cards so that I could study independently when she wasn't there. Mary, my other friend from grad school, helped too. Yet even with their support, I felt like an ant climbing Mount Everest.

How can I possibly pass such a massive exam after what my brain has been through? I thought. I could barely type, and my thoughts weren't clear. And now that I was no longer on medication, I had even lost my ability to dream at night. It was like I was there, but nobody was home. But I had to keep going. I had come too far to give up. So I contacted the school to arrange for extended test taking time and a typist to type my answers while I dictated my response. I then prayed I would pass.

When graduation finally came, it was one of the hottest days in Orange County's history. The glaring sun beat down on us, causing sweat to drip from our brows, and our long black graduation gowns made the heat almost unbearable. I was still in a wheelchair, as I was unable to walk without maximum assistance, so Steven pushed me across the grass, which was not an easy task. He stood in the lineup with me and my fellow students.

"Michelle!" one of them exclaimed. I smiled. Looking at the other students, as they began slowly to recognize me, I noticed a lot of tears in their eyes. There I was on the football field, my long, curly, blond hair gone, replaced by short brown hair covered by a cap, seated in a wheelchair. My voice was still gone and they had to lean in close to hear me. But that didn't matter. Mostly, we just hugged and cried.

As the ceremony began, Tammara was seated on the stage where she would remain until she gave her speech and received her degree. During her speech, she talked about all the sacrifices we made in order to be there that day. The late nights of studying, burning the midnight oil into the wee hours of the morning. All the worry and stress that came for many of us who were balancing work, school, and a family. And that how for some of us, earning this degree had become something so important, that we would fight for our lives to receive it. She then referenced my recent health struggles, telling the crowd of thousands that in spite of my prognosis, I was there that day to walk alongside my classmates.

When all the speeches were said and done, we lined up to walk across the stage, or in my case be wheeled across the stage, shake the college president's hand, and have our picture taken. As I was getting ready to board the wheelchair lift to hoist me onto the platform, I told the operator to stop.

"I'm walking."

"You can't do that," replied the person working the lift.

"Yes, she can," my husband said.

Steven went over to the line-up and grabbed two of the biggest guys he could find, Leroy and Derek, who happened to be African American, both my classmates and my friends. With one man on each arm, we climbed the steps to the top of the stage, and together, the three of us shook the president's hand, gave Tammara a giant hug, and walked off the stage together, accomplishing what I never thought I could.

From then on, life got a little easier. The doctors decided that I didn't need a shunt after all; the water on my brain had resolved on its own. In June, I took the comprehensive exam and passed. Over the summer I even learned how to drive a car again. I was determined to reclaim my life and return to serving my hospice patients. I knew they were the reason God saved me and my continued service to them was absolutely necessary in order to live out God's plan for my life.

In August, I aced my last class before I was mailed my degree and went back to work full-time as the executive director of a hospice foundation. However, the transition from being home and focusing on rehab, to working full-time in a demanding job was overwhelming. I cried nearly every day, I still didn't know how to type well, and I had a difficult time walking. But the change forced me to use my brain again at a critical time in the recovery process. Making decisions, typing letters, running board meetings were all extremely challenging. My self-confidence was low and there were days when I wanted to give up. But I didn't. Instead I tried harder, and deep down, I knew everything would be just fine. My hospice patients needed me.

Another confidence boost came when Hoag Hospital wrote a feature article about my story in their quarterly newsletter, "Scanner," and asked me to be the patient guest of honor at Hoag's 43rd Annual Christmas Carol Ball, which raises money for their Neurosciences Institute. The event was a black tie affair, and I looked absolutely stunning, in my humble opinion. I wore a long, black gown and had my hair and makeup done like a movie star.

When the Master of Ceremonies told how Hoag had removed my once-inoperable lesion after having a catastrophic stroke, I stood from my seat, held the microphone in my good hand, and said, "Thank you to all of the gifted doctors and nurses who saved my life. A special thanks to Dr. Dobkin, who will forever be my angel, and all the people who made my recovery possible."

Dr. Dobkin then stood from his table, dressed in his black tuxedo, came over from across the room, and gave me a giant hug as tears streamed down both of our faces. Together we wept and he kept saying, "You're so beautiful. I can't believe how beautiful you are!"

"Thank you. Thank you for everything," I said as I hugged him tightly. The seated guests rose to their feet, giving us both a standing ovation. My life was in motion, and I was so grateful. And that was the feeling that continued to propel me forward. Gratefulness.

Knowing that we all have a limited amount of time on this earth, I thought about how I could make a bigger difference in my hospice patients' lives. I thought about ways I could help bring them more comfort and more dignity during the most sacred time of life. I thought about my own health struggles and my journey to the *Place of Prayers* where I was one with God, where complete beauty surrounded my soul. And in that moment, I asked God to use me to do his good work. I begged him, in fact. I completely surrendered my life to him and I pleaded for him to use me to help those at the end of life's journey in a powerful and profound way.

My prayer was answered through the creation of the Hospice Angel Assistance Program, a program designed to address the needs of local area individuals facing a terminal illness. Through this program, we provide services that typically are not covered by medical insurances,

Medicare, or MediCal; needs that are largely overlooked in today's healthcare system. Sometimes, these services are as simple as providing transportation. Sometimes, they are as complex as arranging for a child to meet their Hollywood hero before they die. All are equally important, and all speak to the compassion and dignity we seek to provide. Ultimately, our goal is to award patients and their families with meaningful moments that will remain in their hearts forever. And when a request is fulfilled, I give God all the glory, because I know that it is his victory, not mine. I know that ultimately my prayer is being answered; my life's purpose is being fulfilled.

At the end of the day, when I look back and reflect upon all the events in my life, my deepest belief is that *everything* happens for a reason. It's all in God's master plan. James 1:2-3 says, "Consider it pure joy, my brothers and sisters, whenever you face trials of many kinds, because you know that the testing of your faith produces perseverance" (NIV).

It's taken me years to realize that the AVM, which I once thought was a curse, has turned out to be the biggest blessing of my life. And I know that no matter what else happens, no matter what else I'm faced with, no matter how bleak the future may seem, I can always remember that God is at work preparing us for the greater things yet to come. When I trust in him with all my heart, I can be assured that all things can be used for good when we give our lives to him.

EPILOGUE

It's been twenty years since my first stroke and six years since my second stroke. The bedside Christmas tree that once sat next to my hospital bed as a child, and that we planted in the yard, now towers over the two-story home where I grew up. From her kitchen window, my mom has watched the formerly fragile pine grow to be great and powerful. Its strength is a reminder of my strength and it has become a symbol of hope in our household.

Steven and I continue to live in Newport Beach with our dogs, Bear, and newly adopted German Shepard, Bosley. After surviving six rounds of layoffs, Steven is still employed with Starbucks and I continue to serve as executive director to the Southern California Hospice Foundation where I help terminally ill children and adults. Each day I wake, I feel a profound sense of purpose to help those who are nearing the end of life's journey, and it is awesome.

I remain physically disabled with partial paralysis of my right side. I have limited use of my right arm, walk with a limp supported by a leg brace, and have daily bouts of spasticity. This is who I am and I have come to accept my circumstances. Beyond that, Steven and I are currently walking through the process of becoming foster parents, with the hope of one day adopting a child.

All of our trials have made us more appreciative of everything we have. Life is fragile. It can be changed forever in an instant. But believing that everything happens for a reason makes tough transitions a little easier. You can't control what happens to you, but you can control how you react. The choice is yours. Now be brave and become the person you were created to be.

ACKNOWLEDGMENTS

"In everyone's life, at some time, our inner fire goes out. It is then burst into flame by an encounter with another human being. We should all be thankful for those people who rekindle the inner spirit."
—Albert Schweitzer

This book in dedicated to the people who have shaped and molded my life, of which there are many. You will never know how thankful I am to have known you, if even it was just for a little while.

To my husband, Steven, my protector and my soul mate; reliable and strong, honest and sincere. You are everything to me and I love you with all my heart.

A special thanks to my mother who gave me my strength. You are my rock, my biggest fan, and greatest source of support.

To my dear sister Ashley. This experience has strengthened our relationship, bringing us closer together, forming a friendship and love that is as genuine as they come.

To Uncle John, my beloved adviser whose wisdom for life has always inspired me. My admiration for you runs deeper than you will ever know.

To my dearest friend, Christina Galeano. My love for you and your family is the most sincere a friend could ever have.

To my greatest mentor, Kateri Alexander, PhD. Thank you for helping me to find my own way and teaching me how to so eloquently put my thoughts on paper.

To Hamilton School in my hometown of Anza, California. The teachers, the coaches, and the life-long friends have shaped the person I have become. I wouldn't have traded my thirteen years with you for anything.

To the Newport Beach Santa Ana Heights Fire Station #7 who helped to save my life on that fateful January night. You will forever be my heroes.

To the doctors, nurses, and therapists who have helped me along the way, especially Hoag Hospital who worked so hard to assist me in the recovery process after my second stroke. Your tireless work does make a difference.

A heartfelt thanks to my neurosurgeon, William Dobkin, MD. You are my angel and I pray every day that God will continue to use your hands to perform miracles in people's lives.

To my dear friends Tammara Jablonsky and Mary Ellen Blair. Thank you for giving me the strength to finish my master's degree during the weakest moments of my life.

To Terry Ferencik, RN., my first boss out of college and one of the best hospice nurses I have ever met. Thank you for believing in me when it seemed no one else did.

To Shaun Moss, RN, Chris Vallandigham, RN, and Michael Uranga, the founding board members of the Southern California Hospice Foundation. Your presence in my life fills my heart with joy, and I am blessed by your leadership.

To my hospice co-workers and dedicated proofreaders, Judy Russo, Mary Funk, and Lauren Uranga, as well as Professor Dorothy Spirus, who taught the many writing classes I took at the local senior centers. Their gift was encouraging me to just finish.

To my wonderful friend and mentor, Kathi Koll, who cared for her husband, Don, for nearly seven years after he suffered a devastating stroke. You have taught me so much, but perhaps the most important is that "happiness doesn't just happen; it takes a lot of work."

To my literary agent, Mary Keeley. No author can write a book without the support of others. My gratitude goes to you for your guidance and support as I navigated the publishing process.

And finally, to my hospice patients. I can't imagine any other place I would want to be than by your side. Hospice is my ministry and I pray each day that God will continue to use me to do his good work, providing comfort and peace to those at the end of life.

*You can learn more about Michelle Wulfestieg by visiting www. AllWeHaveIsToday.com where you can subscribe to her blogs, follow her on Facebook, or learn about her upcoming speaking engagements.

Made in the USA
San Bernardino, CA
29 February 2020